SWITCH

How 12 Indian Companies
Managed Change Successfully

PRAISE FOR *SWITCH: HOW 12 INDIAN COMPANIES MANAGED CHANGE SUCCESSFULLY*

'As we pass through somewhat trying times, our erstwhile enthusiasm and self-admiration as the second fastest growing economy globally takes some beating and when the general sentiment of apprehension and caution is predominant in the overall business environment, few corporate players have demonstrated their innovativeness of quickly adapting to the change and deriving opportunities out of threats.

L&OD Roundtable, by bringing out *Switch: How 12 Indian Companies Managed Change Successfully*, has done an excellent service for India Inc., as it validates an old aphorism in new style—when the going gets tough, the innovative get going.'

Sudhir Vasudeva, Chairman & Managing Director, ONGC Ltd
'A substantial, important, and transformational book, Dr Banerjee's case studies bring to life Kotter's 8-Step Change Model and provide us with proven examples of successful change despite organizational, market, and industrial challenges. Enormously helpful to both those who are facing change now or will be soon enough!

Marshall Goldsmith, Million-selling author and editor of 32 books, including the *New York Times* bestsellers *MOJO* and *What Got You Here Won't Get You There*
'I congratulate you for such a good documentation of the Change Interventions. I am sure these inspirational stories will make many more organizations and their managers to undertake change interventions and bring pride to their organization, profession and the countries where they are doing business. I am sure this book will be read globally by CEOs, students, managers, teachers, researchers and change facilitators.'

Dr T.V. Rao, Chairman TVRLS and 'The Father of Indian HRD'
'The book is timely and will serve as an excellent resource for both the academic and practising world. As a faculty in the organization and change field both I can see many uses for this volume in both teaching and research. The change journey of each organization included in this volume highlights the challenges that are involved in bringing about change as well as the importance of knowing and understanding the context and being adaptive. As I read each account I felt, "how much it is so much more of the same and yet so different" just as it is true for life and living in general.'

Neharika Vohra, Professor, Organizational Behavior Area, IIM Ahmedabad
'I found myself completely absorbed by the compelling "in the field" stories of leading and managing change in a variety of organizations. Culling what each company did that was distinctive and then sharing the lessons any of us that play a role in transformation should pay attention was simply powerful. This book is a must-read for anyone wanting to understand the art and science of profound change while also considering how to find the best path for an organization's unique journey. I applaud wholeheartedly that this book evolved from thoughtful leaders who wanted to reflect, learn, share and grow as a community.'

Teresa Roche, PhD, Vice President and Chief Learning Officer, Agilent Technologies
'Experience is the best teacher. *Switch: How 12 Indian Companies Managed Change Successfully*, provides an unprecedented opportunity to learn from the experience of twelve successful

change initiatives in one of the world's most dynamic economies. The insights—conveniently summarized at the end of each case—provide enduring lessons for companies faced with the need for change—which, in today's world, includes pretty much everyone.'

Roy V.H. Pollock, DVM, PhD, Chief Learning Officer, The 6Ds Company
'Change does not occur by dreams alone, but also by dogged perseverance in the pursuit of high performance. *Switch* demonstrates that India is well and truly a world-centre for transformational leadership. Every organisation in the book has battled different threats and challenges but they all share an overarching drive to innovate and improve – through shared vision and values, courageous leadership and followership and, most importantly, by investment and development of people. *Switch* is a testament to those who have had the drive and desire to lead change, and is an inspiration to those who aspire to change.'

Stephen Bennett, CEO Inspirational Development Group
'In this remarkable book and actionable guide, Dr Banerjee shows us how to not only predict the future of learning, but create it. This valuable investigation allows us to understand how the most nimble, innovative, and successful organizations throughout Asia navigate—and ultimately lead—change in this turbulent marketplace by developing people at all levels of the organization.

Based on case studies illustrating the leadership practices of the most successful and dynamic organizations operating in Asia, this book is a must-read for anyone working to inspire and grow remarkable leaders for today and tomorrow.'

G. Shawn Hunter, author of *OutThink: How Innovative Leaders Drive Remarkable Outcomes*
'This is an inspiring collection of case studies about inspirational organisational change. Using Kotter's eight principles for managing change effectively, the L&OD roundtable has brought together the twelve best examples of recent change management in Asian organisations. The case studies are written by practitioners, for practitioners and as such provide hands on and real life examples of making change a reality. Well written and comprehensive, I highly recommend this collection for its thoroughness and the way it captures best practice in change management a compelling way.'

Sarah Cook, MD, The Stairway Consultancy Ltd & author of *The Essential Guide to Employee Engagement*
'Sooner or later, all companies face times when they must undergo radical change or close the doors for good. In *Switch*, Dr Banerjee has done us a huge service in highlighting proven, evidence-based success stories that walks us through the entire process of organizational transformation, from identifying the need to implementing and making permanent your new, best practices. Bravo!'

Marshall Goldsmith, Million-selling author and editor of 32 books, including the *New York Times* bestsellers, *MOJO* and *What Got You Here Won't Get You There*

SWITCH

How 12 Indian Companies
Managed Change Successfully

Sujaya Banerjee

Founder—L&OD Roundtable

Chief Talent Officer & Senior Vice President HR, Essar

B L O O M S B U R Y

NEW DELHI • LONDON • OXFORD • NEW YORK • SYDNEY

BLOOMSBURY INDIA
Bloomsbury Publishing India Pvt. Ltd
Second Floor, LSC Building No. 4, DDA Complex, Pocket C – 6 & 7,
Vasant Kunj, New Delhi, 110070

BLOOMSBURY, BLOOMSBURY INDIA and the Diana logo
are trademarks of Bloomsbury Publishing Plc

First published in India 2014
This edition published 2014

Copyright © 2014 Bloomsbury Publishing India Pvt Ltd

This book is solely the responsibility of the author and the publisher has had no
role in the creation of the content and does not have responsibility for anything
defamatory or libellous or objectionable

ISBN: PB: 978-93-82951-52-0
2 4 6 8 10 9 7 5 3

Typeset by Eleven Arts
Printed in India by Manipal Technologies Limited, Manipal

To find out more about our authors and books visit www.bloomsbury.com
and sign up for our newsletters

CONTENTS

ACKNOWLEDGMENTS

This book is a result of the vision and passion of many Leaders. The Governing Council of the Learning and OD Roundtable, who had the vision to recognise that the Learning & OD Community had come of age; needed a voice through a forum that exchanged stories, ideas, best practices and built capabilities to become true Learning Organisations so as to leverage the opportunities of our times.

This book is undoubtedly a celebration of the rigour, astuteness, sweat and strife of all the stellar organisations which came forth to share their incredible stories of change and the twelve organisations that finally won over our discerning Jury members as the best examples of change.

Our heartfelt gratitude for the contributions made by the following outstanding professionals from the winning organisations, who made the effort to share their stories with great enthusiasm. This book is based on entries at the Best Change Interventions of Asia Study presented by these Change Leaders (in alphabetical order):

- Capgemini—Rajesh Padmanabhan and Gayathri Ramamurthy
- Dr Reddy's Laboratories Ltd—Padma Rajeswari Tata and Joel Chandra
- GVK MIAL—Manoj Rajimwale
- HPCL Mittal Energy Ltd.—Ashok Kumar and Girish H

- Lafarge India Pvt. Ltd.—Aparna Sharma

- Mahindra & Mahindra Ltd—Prince Augustin and Naushad Noorani

- PNB Housing Finance Ltd—Anshul Bhargava and Satish Singh

- SAIL—Manas Ranjan Panda and Sanjay Dhar

- Tata Motors Ltd—Prabir Jha and Vineet Soni

- Wartsila India Ltd.—Usha Venkatesh

- Wipro Ltd.—Sarika Pradhan Jena, Shveta Srivastava and Namita Shriwastav

- Zensar Technologies Ltd.—Ruchi Mathur and Janki Sampat

Thanks to Ester Martinez of People Matters for the help in publicising the study, the distinguished Jury for investing the time and seriousness in assessing the entries.

And last but importantly, the L&OD Roundtable Team which has worked tirelessly to help execute the idea of the Best Change Interventions of Asia Study 2012/2013 and compile this book to share these fascinating stories of Change with the rest of the world. Anand Justin Cherian and Gaurav Mukherjee you are both stars!

My heartfelt gratitude to all for enabling this professionally fulfilling and personally transforming experience for me. Your Passion, Leadership and Versatility are truly humbling.

Dr Sujaya Banerjee
Founder—L&OD Roundtable

PREFACE

This journey called the L&OD Roundtable began four years ago and was conceived as a community of like-minded professionals in the area of Strategic HR, Learning & OD coming to learn and grow together. The objective was to create a much needed platform for enabling meaningful conversation and dialogues on the core challenges organisations were experiencing and how Learning & OD professionals could contribute effectively to the change agendas emerging within their organisations.

The Roundtable was created to serve as a knowledge-sharing and practice building platform for facilitating dialogue, building capabilities and sharing resources. The last two decades of continuous change in India has created huge opportunities for developing indigenous knowledge and models that work in the Indian context using key cultural levers for driving change successfully. The L&OD Roundtable aspires to capture this knowledge and make it available to member organisations as experiences, cases and stories that are contextually relevant as compared to the overdependence on western stories, cases, examples and models as done currently.

Towards this end, the L&OD Roundtable has undertaken two pioneering studies—The Best Learning Organisations of Asia Study in 2011/2012 and now the Best Change Interventions of Asia Study 2012/2013, which attempted to capture the Best Transformation Stories in India Inc.

This book is the outcome of this study undertaken in 2012/2013 culminating in the Best Change Interventions of Asia Seminar and Awards in 2013. We initiated the study by inviting companies to share their most successful transformation story. The task was challenging as the entry was to be submitted by stacking the key components of each change story to Kotter's Eight Step Process for Leading Change. All entries invited needed to describe the change intervention in the context of measures taken towards:

1. Creating urgency around a vision for change

2. Operationalising the change

3. Designing a communication strategy and ensuring sound feedback mechanisms.

4. Managing initial resistance and leveraging early wins to build momentum.

5. Institutionalising the change to ensure it sticks

Forty-two organisations expressed their interest, twenty-two managed to send stories that could finally stack up to the stringent criteria set for the entries and twelve organisations finally made it to the final list of winning organisations. This included organisations like Capgemini, Dr Reddy's, GVK, HMEL, Lafarge, Mahindra & Mahindra Ltd, PNB Housing Finance Ltd, SAIL, Tata Motors, Wartsila, Wipro and Zensar which are presented in this book.

An eminent Jury comprising of Dr TV Rao (Chairman—TVRLS and ex-Dean—Indian Institute of Management (IIM) Ahmedabad) , Anil Sachdev (Founder—School of Inspired Leadership), P Thiruvengadam (Sr Director Deloitte), Prof. S Ramnarayan (Clinical Professor—Indian School of Business) and Dr Kishore Dash (Associate Professor—Thunderbird School of Global Management) judged the entries which were shared with an audience of over 250 HR/ Learning and OD Professionals at the Best Change Interventions of Asia (BCIA) Seminar and Awards, held in July 2013.

The Best Change Interventions of Asia platform was an opportunity to capture stories of Courage, Leadership and Conviction. The idea was to inspire members to take on the mantle of change fearlessly.

This book presents the twelve winning entries and our objective remains to inspire professionals to build courage to become the voice of change and transformation, to identify opportunities and support the organisation to push the needle, raise the bar, build the competence of Change Management and help build Learning Organisations.

Each story in this book is a real life story of identifying the need to change, rallying support for the change, managing resistance, influencing and communicating the change and triumphing by institutionalising the change successfully.

We hope this book serves as a reminder to all, of the vast reservoir of resources within us to create a better world. Managing change is also easily the most wanted/ needed competence for Transforming India.

Change Fast, Learn Faster..........

INTRODUC-TION:

Two decades of continuing transformation

The India Change Story

India's remarkable progress particularly over the last two decades made it the vortex of continuing change as industries, entrepreneurs and professionals geared up to leverage the many opportunities that became available.

While the genesis of this transformation is rooted in reforms initiated post Liberalization in the nineties, the virtuous cycle of growth that ensured has been mainly the result of great Indian entrepreneurship. A major shift in the economy also saw a strong service sector emerge with the growth of sunrise industries like the IT, ITES companies and the nudging out of the traditional Pharmaceutical and Automobile sectors.

THE VIRTUOUS CYCLE OF GROWTH

India has the unique distinction of crossing the per capita GDP levels of US $ 500 and US $ 1000 in the same decade. Needless to say this has had great implications for consumption demand and finance with investment and savings rapidly growing within the economy.

The service sector boomed as the demand for homes, consumer goods, financial services and other goods and services went up. This in turn drove the upward migration of incomes which drove more economic activity. India quickly adopted information and communication technology— leapfrogging many intermediate steps in the evolution of technology. This enabled the scaling up of new paradigms of distribution and service delivery in a wide range of areas.

Technology has pervaded every aspect of economic activity in India. The rise of communications technology has been particularly significant with the spectacular growth of mobile telephony and increased connectivity. India is home to the third largest internet user base at ten million users and the second largest mobile subscriber base of over 800 million. Infrastructure is a key growth area for the economy—it offers opportunities in several sectors including building of highways, ports, airports, telecommunications, urban infrastructure, power, railways and oil and gas. There has been an estimated investment of USD one trillion in infrastructure with fifty per cent of this coming from private sectors and public-private partnership. This level of infrastructural investment has had a significantly positive impact on economic growth, demand for output, generation of employment and improvement of national productivity.

POISED FOR TRULY EXCITING TIMES

India is poised for a great future ahead with more opportunities and challenges emerging with India's growth story. The aspirations of a young population coupled with a growing Corporate Sector and the disruptive import of Technology is unveiling a truly exciting journey ahead. Corporates continue to play an important part in the journey of enabling India to realise its true potential.

In order to sustain the momentum the key priorities for the economy must include investment and capital formation, increasing agricultural output, control over deficits and improvement in education and skill building. Corporates can significantly play a role in the area of skill-building and capability development .Even though ninety per cent of entry level talent in the workforce are literate today, the institutional capacity for providing skills training is very inadequate. Skill enhancement to meet the requirements of industry require both private and public sector to contribute in the area of capability building and enhancement of talent.

NEW INSIGHTS FOR MANAGING CHANGE IN A NEW WORLD

We have seen a new world emerge around us in the past two decades in India and we are increasingly experiencing a world of new opportunities and challenges.

Fuelled by growth, affluence is fast gathering pace with greater aspirations and consumerism than ever before. It's a whole new India to be living and working for experienced by the Managers/ Corporate Leaders today. Talent dynamics in the market place are changing the power equation between Employers and Employees in a significant way. As opportunities and aspirations grow, Corporates are experiencing a new challenge of retention and delivering on their value propositions.

Constant technological innovations have lead to an ever evolving workplace that will need to keep pace in order to stay ahead of competition. Global connectivity in the workplace is both a necessity and a norm and will continue to drive discontinuous change and be a game changer for Corporates that are more agile to adopt and imbibe technology as an edge.

"Managing change" has not surprisingly emerged as a key Leadership competence and those who possess the ability to initiate and manage change are undoubtedly the most sought after talent. Managing an organisation in a constantly evolving environment is a challenging task that will need new insights to understand and interpret the interconnectedness among seemingly exclusive parameters. Sound decision making is the need of the hour, the ability to de-clutter the mind, see data in perspective, having the ability to analyse both quantitative and qualitative data for managing change effectively are all key.

As we talk about a turbulent changing macro environment it is important to acknowledge that as knowledge will turn obsolete in a fast changing environment, it is imperative for organisations to invest in a continuous learning process to ensure their talent is at the cutting edge. Building Learning organisations that have a structured learning agenda with well-established knowledge management and knowledge-transfer platforms are crucial for remaining at the cutting-edge. Building the ability to handle discordant information and act on feedback is key to ensure organisational renewal mechanisms are in place to truly become Learning organisations. The sum total of knowledge inside an organisation must exceed the sum total of change outside to enable organisations to remain truly competitive.

MULTIPLE PILLARS FOR GROWTH, MULTIPLE LEVERS FOR CHANGE

The India growth story is built on multiple pillars that have enabled its success over the past two decades .Consumption technologies will continue to have a disruptive influence as India continues to grow. There will also be significant opportunities to leverage technology to drive new business models in the future.

Managers in India have experienced significant changes in the workplace not only because of the apparent demographic changes within the talent pool, but because it is imperative to engage in a continuous process of skill enhancement , sound decision making skills, a never ending penchant to learn as discontinuous change becomes the way of life for Indian Managers.

Identifying the levers for change and navigating the organisation through change agendas successfully are key in these exciting times.

THE L&OD ROUNDTABLE – THE BEST CHANGE INTERVENTIONS OF ASIA STUDY 2012–13

The Learning & OD Roundtable, a not-for-profit forum of Strategic HR/ Learning and OD practitioners was a forum created in 2011 to enable capability building and to help organisations drive change and Learning effectively to become Learning organisations.

In 2012 The L&OD Roundtable initiated the Best Change Interventions of Asia study to capture some of these exciting stories of Transformation that organisations in India Inc. would now have the opportunity to document and share with the world.

The idea was to invite the Best Change stories and understand how change was being lead and managed within these organisations

WHAT TRANSFORMATION LEADERS DO DIFFERENTLY TO ENSURE CHANGE EFFORTS SUCCEED

We first explored what 'Transformation Leaders' do differently to ensure that change efforts sustain and succeed. This was then used as the framework for assessing the 'Best Change Stories' at the Best Change Interventions of Asia Study 2012/2013. We referred to John Kotter's pioneering work 'Leading Change' which is easily the best guide for managing change effectively.

1. **Transformation Leaders identify a Burning platform for change and build a keen sense of urgency around the change efforts**. They bring people out of their comfort zones to focus on areas of vulnerability for the organisation—like competition, flat earnings, decreasing market share or losing talent. Change management efforts usually fail unless the organisation is able to build a sense of urgency where at least seventy-five per cent of the leaders believe that doing business as usual is not going to give them new results.

2. **Transformation Leaders create a group of change sponsors:** Sponsors are managers and supervisors who ensure that everyone does what is necessary to accomplish the change. This group must contribute to experiences which can further drive change efforts, team cognition and energies in the right direction. Transformation Leaders build 'Coalitions of Influencers' who help drive change and manage naysayers and early resistance effectively.

3. **Transformation Leaders create a vision for change**—It is key to create and define an-easy-to-understand vision that helps test the rationale for change and keep all change efforts aligned. It is imperative that the vision for change is easily comprehended and communicated to all.

4. **Transformation Leaders engage through communication**— Transformation Leaders are great at advocating the vision for change and evangelising it throughout the organisation. The communication process has to be exhaustive in this regard. Most people must understand and appreciate the change in order to participate, appreciate and remain committed to the reason for change.

5. **Transformation Leaders know that People Empowerment is key:** They encourage their organisations to remain agile by encouraging employees to participate in decision making. This is not the same as having the authority to make decisions. There is a difference between delegating and empowering. Delegating is the act of giving someone else the authority to make decisions specific to an assignment or a point in time. Empowerment on the other hand is the process through which power is mutually shared. 'Empowerment' is a trendy management jargon and often a contemporary expectation from Leadership of our times. However it must be preceded by education, coaching, training and management of consequences of decision making.

6. **Transformation Leaders celebrate early successes and wins:** They ensure that short term wins or early signs of progress are communicated and celebrated to keep the energies around the change initiatives going. They understand that real transformation efforts take time and there can easily be a loss of momentum and early onset of disappointments unless people see evidence of their efforts bearing fruits. When people realise that real change takes a long time the urgency around the change efforts may drop and the intensity and efforts may get reduced. It is therefore imperative to keep the motivation for change going while using the opportunities to reflect and revisit the vision for change

7. **Transformation Leaders keep a continuous improvement focus to change**—They know that their efforts will take a while and explore changes in the basic culture of the organisation. This is to explore the systems relationships within organisations which may need some tuning before moving people committed to doing things in a new way to perform new roles. Until change efforts sink in deeply into the organisation's 'way of doing things' all change efforts are fragile and susceptible to regressing back to old ways. Change champions understand this well and use early wins to delve deeper into cultural issues which may adversely impact the sustenance of change efforts.

8. **Transformation Leaders ensure Behaviour-Based not Activity-Based change**—Change must finally impact 'the way in which we do things around here'—the culture of the organisation. Transformation Leaders acknowledge this and until change efforts are rooted in the social norms and shared values of the organisation, they remain superficial and are subject to retracting to the old ways under pressure. Transformation Leaders help people make connections between efforts and outcomes and get the correlation. Change sponsors embody the new ways so that that employees adopt and remain committed to the new approaches, behaviours and attitudes that can help the organisation achieve its vision for change

THE CHANGE TRAP: WHAT COMES FIRST—PREPAREDNESS TO CHANGE OR THE CHANGE?

This has been an existential question for many Change Champions and all of us know Heraclitus quoted in the sixth century BC that, "the only constant is change." Despite this, organisations find themselves entrapped in the belief that they need to prepare by investing resources, time and energy preparing for change rather than achieving its desired outcomes.

Even with the pressures of turbulent times some organisations recognise the need to change, create a vision for change but go about meticulously preparing the organisation for the change, rooted in the belief that the Organisation's readiness is key to successful change efforts. Transformation Leaders demonstrate boldness and new ways of thinking and acting. They demand the outcomes be achieved quickly with a sense of urgency—not after months and years of finally becoming "ready" for change.

When Leaders focus on the desired outcomes (vision for change) and make requests for rapid advancements, two things happen:

1. The organisation responds faster by achieving early wins, improving performance and building confidence

2. These initial successes demonstrate what can actually work and helps build credibility, making longer term changes possible in systems, structures and processes by making them more effective.

CHANGE LEADERS? CHANGE MANAGERS?

This question has always loomed large as I am sure it has for others who initiate change efforts within their organisations. The general belief is that successful change efforts need Strategic Visionaries who can study the macro environment, identify the business case for change and create the change vision for the organisation to gain a competitive edge (price advantage, product innovation, customer satisfaction).

Strategic capabilities versus Execution/Managerial prowess is a strong debate on deciphering the style and approach of a successful transformation champion. If both visionary strategic leadership and managerial capabilities are found wanting—change efforts go nowhere.

TRANSFORMATION LEADERS AND THE PEOPLE FACTOR

Change is tough to handle, is unpredictable and demanding. It can shake up people and generate fear that can threaten the success of the organisation in the marketplace.

Building organisations that are agile and nimble to manage change involves—being quick to market by designing and delivering more creative solutions for the customers, developing new business while retaining existing customers. Transformation Leaders hire and retain people who are resourceful, motivated and focused on ensuring the success of the organisation at all times.

They ensure people know and understand the boundaries and know how to work within them while challenging the system, understanding the dynamics of change but coming to expect the unexpected at all times.

Building agile organisations and people resilience is key in today's era of perpetual unrest. Employers must be prepared to handle the relentless and complex changes that are prevalent and flooding the marketplace and the business. The trick is to remain change-ready and constantly challenge the status-quo. To succeed in unpredictable environments organisations need to be nimble. Nimbleness is the ability to consistently succeed in unpredictable environments by implementing changes more effectively and efficiently than the competition and being prepared to pro-actively drive change to achieve greater success. The alternative of remaining still does not exist. Transformation Leaders drive their energies for managing change, successfully rooted in the wisdom that the *price of doing nothing is Failure*.

We set out to validate all this by inviting organisations within India Inc. to participate by describing their successful transformation stories to us.

The twelve best stories that stacked up to our Best Change Interventions of Asia template (see the chapter 'About the Best Change Interventions of Asia Study'), based on John Kotter's 8 Step Process for Leading Change. The forthcoming chapters feature one such change story each. Each chapter features the context for envisioning the change, operationalising the change, designing a communication strategy for change, managing initial resistance and leveraging early wins, institutionalising the change and finally the impact of the change intervention on the organisation. Don't miss the Box elucidating what the organisation did differently for managing change successfully, and also the Box on Key Lessons for Change Managers.

This book promises to be a treat for Leaders who are passionate about change, offering a plethora of insights through terrains of different industries, looking at how organisations engaged with their unique challenges in order to generate and execute meaningful solutions by influencing key organisational levers, managing resistance, providing momentum to their change agendas and finally delivering positive impact. Get ready to be charged with new ideas, innovative solutions and insights to create your own armoury of Change Management

CHANGE TO ANSWER A TIMELY EXISTENTIAL QUESTION

The Capgemini Story

"The rate of change is not going to slow down anytime soon. If anything, competition in most industries will probably speed up even more in the next few decades."

—John P. Kotter

COMPANY PROFILE

Capgemini
CONSULTING.TECHNOLOGY.OUTSOURCING

EXCELL EXecutive CEnter
for Leadership Learning

With more than 1,25,000 people in forty-four countries, Capgemini is one of the world's foremost providers of consulting, technology and outsourcing services in the world. Capgemini Global reported 2012 global revenues of EUR 10.3 billion (more than $13 billion USD). A deeply multicultural organisation, Capgemini has developed its own way of working, the Collaborative Business Experience™ . Collaborative Business Experience TM : Cloud-based, ERP independent, e-Procurement consulting offering at Capgemini . It draws on Rightshore®, its worldwide delivery model.

Capgemini in India is around 42,000 people strong across nine cities (Mumbai, Delhi, Bangalore, Hyderabad, Pune, Kolkata and Chennai, Trichy and Salem). With dedicated teams to service the local markets, Capgemini has strong domain experience to assist clients across the Government and Public Sector, Energy and Utilities, Manufacturing, Telecom and Financial Services sectors and help them advance in their respective industries.

Capgemini espouses an inspiring Vision statement—*Enabling Freedom*, referring to the organisation's fundamental motivation and drive towards providing clients with insights and capabilities intended to boost their freedom to realise superior results. *Enabling Business Transformation*, is the Mission statement, revealing just how it intends to achieve its vision, as also the targeted level and impact of its contribution to the success of client organisations.

CAPGEMINI INDIA—EVOLVING FOR FUTURE NEEDS

The India organisation found itself at an interesting juncture, with business and Capgemini Global forces coming together as they did, circa 2011. Fittingly enough, the question looming over the organisation was—'How do we enable the freedom of *our own* organisation, Capgemini India Pvt. Ltd.?'

With an astute awareness of a dynamic business environment punctuated by macroeconomic uncertainty, stiff external competition and growing customer expectations; the organisation embarked on its change journey, knowing that these compelling imperatives demanded key capabilities in top and middle management levels. In the context of this environment, the expectation from the India organisation was clear: to move from being a delivery offshore centre to creating value with an end-to-end business model. What was also clear was that such a transformation would require necessary changes not just in processes and portfolios, but more importantly also changes in mind-set. Leaders would now need to think differently, with a more strategic, holistic perspective; building learning agility not just for themselves, but also for the organisations they lead.

With leaders being responsible for defining the strategy, devising the execution plan and enabling performance and engagement; their role in bringing about this transformation and achieving business outcomes was critical. The organisation therefore focused on its leaders in terms of developing capabilities and perspectives to achieve the desired change.

ENVISIONING THE REQUIRED CHANGE

In early 2011, Capgemini Global set the 2015 Vision, elucidated succinctly as:

- Increase gross operating margin
- Double global revenues

With clear objectives set for 2012 and 2013 to guide the organisation towards the 2015—Vision, Capgemini India strongly believed in the key role that leadership effectiveness would play in the achievement of these growth objectives. Dipping into management research reinforced and re-validated their view on the importance of developing competencies at the senior executive level for substantive organisational growth.

With this commitment and the aim of building a leadership pool ready to contribute to the needs of not just the evolving India organisation, but of Capgemini Global as well, EXCELL(Executive Centre for Leadership Learning) was launched. Targeted at the Vice President level, EXCELL was designed to help enhance performance effectiveness by leveraging existing capabilities and working on areas of development through customised interventions. A simple, uncomplicated value proposition was identified for every program stakeholder, in order to clarify respective roles in the larger scheme of things, as well as the benefits that would accrue from such an intervention.

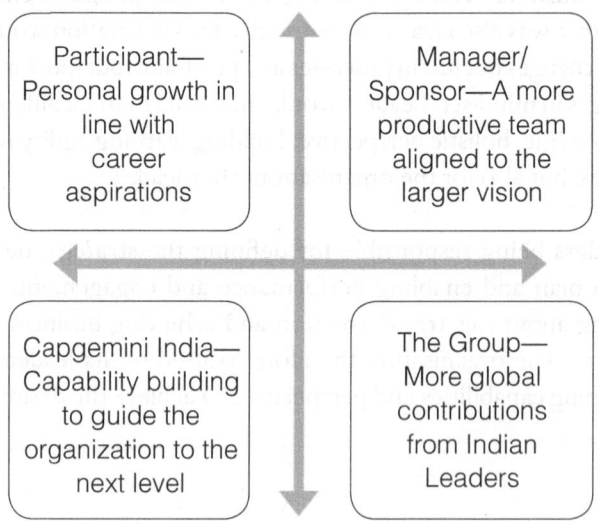

EXCELL Pre-Diagnostics: Stakeholder Expectations

In the design stage itself, the EXCELL Vision was shared with key stakeholders, with a view to evolve a collaborative idea around the initiative. The all important 'What's in it for me' was addressed through dedicated sensitization and orientation sessions.

The vision had been articulated in a manner that showed the intuitive linkages to the larger organisational goal and how that in turn fit in the Capgemini Global level scheme of things (2015 Vision). This was followed by detailed Diagnostic and Development phases, briefly described below:

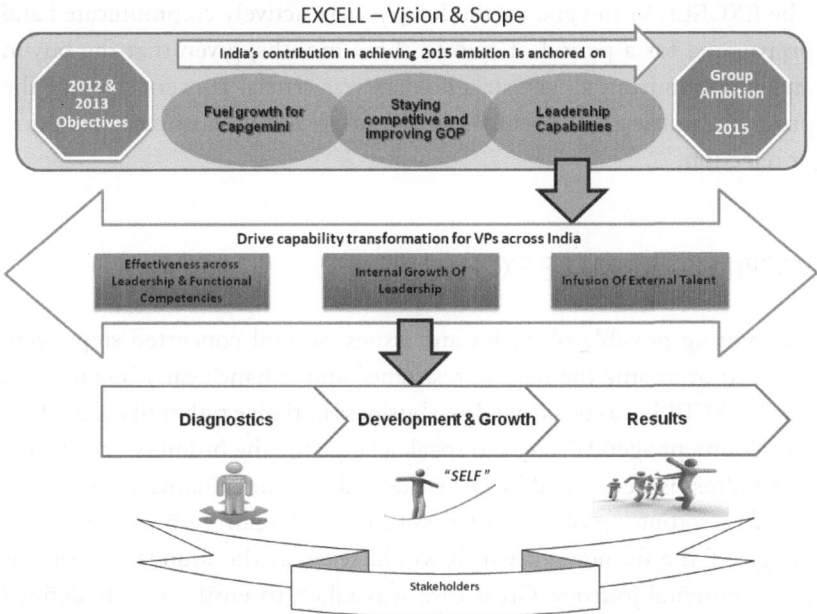

Within the figure:

EXCELL – Vision & Scope

India's contribution in achieving 2015 ambition is anchored on

2012 & 2013 Objectives

Fuel growth for Capgemini

Staying competitive and improving GOP

Leadership Capabilities

Group Ambition 2015

Drive capability transformation for VPs across India

Effectiveness across Leadership & Functional Competencies

Internal Growth Of Leadership

Infusion Of External Talent

Diagnostics | Development & Growth | Results

"SELF"

Stakeholders

The EXCELL Vision and Scope

Diagnostic phase: In this phase the organisation partnered with a reputed firm in the area of leadership assessment and carried out a series of diagnostics including Psychometric Testing, Cognitive Abilities Functioning and Experience Profiling. In addition to these, Capgemini India also deployed multi-rater feedback to provide a holistic, multi-faceted view of leaders. In the next step, leaders were mapped on a Nine-box Performance— Potential grid basis the diagnostic results, which were analysed in-depth to effectively map areas of participants' strength and development and identify opportunities and roadblocks for individual development. Each leader also received an Individual Development Plan, which would form the core of the development process that followed.

Development Phase: This focused on executing a personalised development program for each leader based on the specific findings of the diagnostic, with mechanisms for quarterly review of progress made. A wide array of developmental avenues was deployed to maximise the effectiveness of the intervention, including Instructor-led Learning Programs, One-the-Job Learning, Action Learning Programs, Executive Coaching and Self-driven learning. These development interventions were dove-tailed into the competencies to identify and address specific learning needs.

The EXCELL Vision and methodology were actively communicated and propagated for a period of two to three months, given that the buy-in and adoption from all key stakeholders was crucial at every stage of the program, not least of all in the make-or-break phase of early adoption or rejection.

WORKING TO MAKE EXCELL A REALITY

Preempting possible obstacles and issues, several concerted steps were taken to overcome the natural resistance and enhance early buy-in. First of all, EXCELL was positioned as a business initiative rather than an HR or 'development agenda', so as to speak a language the business understood and address issues valued by key stakeholders. The initiative commenced with the setting up of a core Cross-functional Team responsible for the design of the framework which would serve as the foundation for this developmental journey. Great care was taken to ensure clearly defined responsibilities were in place for all stakeholders in the EXCELL program. The team set about creating a 'Capgemini design'—a framework tailor-made for the transformational needs envisaged towards achieving the 2015 Vision. This was crystallised through Focused Group Discussions conducted across Business Units, designed to gauge challenges experienced and arising expectations from the Leadership Development program—the needs, outcomes, metrics, and methodology.

This strong drive towards the involvement of leaders from the very beginning, served also to clarify and set the context for desired outcomes. The aim was to keep the 'Self', i.e. the participants themselves, at the core of the engine that would drive this program forward.

Key leaders and stakeholders from across Business Units were involved in the program design and roll-out right from the start. Apart from engaging experienced HR professionals, from the India organisation and beyond, the team also tapped into the expertise of the Capgemini University based in Paris, a central provider of learning solutions to Capgemini Global. When it came to execution, Capgemini partnered with proven experts in the leadership development space to make sure they got it right the first time.

One of the key components of the Diagnostic process was the Multi-Rater Perception Survey, covering a diverse sample of respondents for every leader; including the participant, his/her supervisor, the service line leader, team members, peers and even external customers. This was designed in view of the collaboration and teamwork necessary for success in a multi-geographic, multi-cultural environment like that of Capgemini. The metrics for measuring development were continuously refined basis inputs from Business stakeholders across levels, who displayed great commitment to the initiative.

It was felt that the impact of the development and change would need to be experienced across a larger audience for it to be sustainable. Thus, while EXCELL primarily targeted the Vice President population, employees upto one or two levels lower were covered under EXCELL Lite, with corresponding diagnostics and development interventions. The program was designed bearing in mind that while the overarching leadership competencies might be similar across levels, their definition in terms of proficiency and also the behavioural indicators would certainly vary.

At the time of printing, the team was in the process of extending the development program forward, to cover the core leadership team—the Business Units and Support Heads, under what has been christened EXCELL ++. This should serve to complete the envisioned plan of developing critical capabilities across leadership levels; to maximise organisational performance.

ENSURING 2-WAY COMMUNICATION TO DRIVE CHANGE EFFECTIVELY

The program participants were from diverse backgrounds, covering customer facing roles, Subject Matter Experts, Functional Leads and Support Leads. It was important to customise the program based on specific needs so as to enhance the relevance, consequent buy-in, and most importantly, end impact of the development efforts. Inputs from the multi-rater instrument were used to help segregate learning needs in the Diagnostic phase.

An important development need that emerged through the diagnostics and in Individual Development Plans was People Leadership skills. Coaching workshops were conducted for leaders to equip and empower them as coaches for identified High Potential High Performer employee segments in their respective business units. This workshop was designed to foster employee engagement while continually enhancing the performance levels of participants. It also aimed at developing pipeline strength with succession plans for critical positions, supporting career development within the organisation and driving change and building advocacy for the overarching 2015 Vision.

As with any effective long-term initiative, feedback mechanisms for continuous improvement were an integral part of EXCELL. Quarterly Development Review meetings were organised with participants to gauge progress made in their specific development activities. The team also reported back to the business sponsors regularly to integrate their inputs back into the program. Feedback was also collected using a custom-designed feedback form at the end of every workshop, which helped garner inputs to refine processes and systems further. Improvements on the multi-rater instrument and even the extension of EXCELL to EXCELL Lite and EXCEL ++, were outcomes of analysing and acting on feedback received through this often underrated channel.

BUILDING MOMENTUM TO COUNTER THE RESISTANCE TO CHANGE

Every step of the change intervention held the potential for resistance. The Diagnostics by themselves could have triggered anxieties which were countered proactively with an open and transparent communication strategy. There was significant resistance experienced from key influencers within Business Units. The discomfort was on multiple fronts—prohibitive costs, lengthy processes, skepticism on the need/ relevance of such a program and the like. Also, investing time in an extended program with long-term outcomes presented natural challenges in terms of buy-in and adoption.

The team embarked on a phase-wise approach to countering the resistance. All Business Units were covered during the first (Diagnostic) phase of the program, which was run as the pilot batch. Selling the proposition to this first batch was, without doubt, the most critical step in silencing naysayers and in fact bringing them over to the side for change. Familiarization meetings were held with participants on the Diagnostics phase to discuss both the content and process with timelines for completion. This reinforced the involvement of the 'Self' in one's own development. Awareness meetings were held with supervisors on process, content, outcomes and the support required to ensure success, along with orientation sessions on the Multi-Rater Instrument for the Perception Survey, detailing the design and purpose behind the same. Efforts were made with the learning partner to fine tune the Diagnostic Design, enhancing organisational fit.

**"Awareness → Acceptance → Action"
model to overcome resistance**

Moving from mind-set change to process change

Post Diagnostics completion, detailed feedback was collected from participants on ways to improve the participant experience and process efficacy, resulting in modifications in tool administration as well as fine-tuning of the overall process design.

A particular Business Unit was categorically in denial of the entire intervention, forcing the team to think beyond the original plan and take a different route to influence their buy-in. Firstly, they were given a special, detailed orientation on the process, its context, and expected outcomes for the organisation in the coming years.

Winning over the pilot batch participants was the clincher, with the positive decibels spreading across Business Units and locations. Even while the program was branded internally and forums created to enable open sharing of opinions and feedback, the word-of-mouth publicity, which only real quality and efficacy can bring about, remained the most powerful vindication and advertisement of the adopted approach.

INSTITUTIONALISING THE CHANGE TO ACCOMPLISH THE VISION

Institutionalising the program was a prime consideration for the team throughout—from design to execution to refinement, the focus always was on ensuring stability and continuity by means of documentation, review mechanisms with key stakeholders and integration with other people processes. Based on the early wins, it was decided to broad-base the program by extending it to both the senior executive leadership (EXCELL++) as well as potential leadership successors (EXCELL Lite). Through these carefully designed interventions, the organisation aimed to make the EXCELL vision sustainable, embedding it as an integral part of the leadership and cultural fabric of the organisation, aligned meaningfully with key business imperatives.

Even with the success achieved thus far, the team remains conscious of the ground left to be covered as far as complete institutionalization goes. The plan is to focus on process automation to the extent possible, to enhance its robustness and resilience to changes in personnel and administration. There have been detailed interactions and orientations with the HR Business Partners, to equip them to effectively support participants in their development journey.

Additionally, EXCELL forms an important part of the induction of both laterally hired and internally promoted Vice Presidents. This induction focuses on the key objectives of the organisation and the ways and means to leverage their individual leadership capabilities to further Capgemini's growth story.

IMPACT ON THE ORGANISATION

At the time of printing, forty-nine Vice President participants had been covered as part of the EXCELL program (nearly fifty per cent of the leadership), with plans to cover fifty emerging leaders and Senior Vice Presidents through the EXCELL Lite and EXCELL++ interventions, within the following two quarters.

Even with a measured, modest start, there have been some commendable achievements made along the way. As described previously, post diagnostics participants are mapped on the Nine-box Performance—Potential grid for development purposes, presenting a snapshot of where they lie currently. Through the customised interventions deployed thus far, over seventy per cent of the participants have displayed significant/moderate development progress.

The team has identified two levels of inputs to ascertain the development achieved by a leader. Firstly, the weighted average of the performance ratings over the past three years with weights increasing with recency and secondly, a multi-rater questionnaire to assess the leader's proficiency on leadership competencies. Metrics considered include both business and people leadership aspects of performance. These inputs then guide decisions on accelerating development and increasing the impact and efficacy of development interventions.

The leadership coaching program also provided the organisation the opportunity to involve high potential women coachees, which served the dual purpose of Leadership Pipelining and the Diversity and Inclusion agenda.

EXCELL has successfully enabled the organisation to strengthen its leadership capability, both at senior levels as well as in the pipeline for a sustainable future. The HR capabilities have increased multifold in the process as well. Following are the long-term strategic benefits that the organisation is working to derive from the EXCELL program:

> For me as a coach, the process has been equally enriching where I have developed my own listening skills and overall agility in looking for coachable aha moments which bring a smile on my coachees' faces."
>
> —Ashutosh Misra (Head of Operations, Group Sales, Capgemini)

- Transformation of Leadership landscape with due focus on balancing internal capabilities with external talent

- Top-down approach to foster a development culture in the organisation

- A continuous learning culture across leadership levels, enabling a Tech Major such as Capgemini to remain agile in a dynamic business environment

EXCELL at Capgemini is among those exemplary processes that have successfully knitted together the people agenda with the business case, to the extent of equating the two given that the most sustainable differentiator between organisations remains Talent.

This chapter is based on the entry submitted by Rajesh Padmanabhan (Corporate Vice President & CHRO, Capgemini) and Gayathri Ramamurthy (Associate Director—Leadership Development and D&I Lead, Capgemini) at the Best Change Interventions of Asia Study 2012

What Capgemini did differently to successfully manage and drive change

The Capgemini story looks at how a regional organisation prepared itself to take on evolved, global responsibilities. The following were some of the key highlights of the change effort:

- Branching out EXCELL to EXCELL Lite (For next two level leaders) and EXCELL++ (For the Executive Leadership Team) ensured that a wide enough spectrum of influencers and key stakeholders were made an active part of the change. This would certainly have helped in overcoming resistance, and enabling faster internalization of the change within the organisation.

- The Coaching Workshops sought to enhance employee engagement and commitment, and strengthen the leadership pipeline, which were key ingredients in realising the desired change. This awareness of strengthening vital change enablers whilst retaining the focus on the main change initiative (EXCELL) was an important aspect of the change effort at Capgemini.

Lessons for Change Managers

The Capgemini EXCELL story presents several valuable lessons for Change Managers, irrespective of industry sector and organisation size:

- From the very outset, the all important 'What's in it for ME?' was clarified and communicated to all process stakeholders. This was key not only in enhancing their commitment and buy-in, but also served to demystify the entire change agenda, which can often be intimidating when unclear.

- Basing the change as a natural requisite for the overarching business goal helps in garnering support and alignment across levels. In Capgemini's case, the 2015 Vision served to lend the entire effort a sense of direction, while galvanising all stakeholders towards the common organisational aim.

- The importance of investing efforts in identifying the unique needs of the organisation in the current context and customising change efforts accordingly can never be overstated.

REVAMPING TALENT ACQUISITION PROGRAMS FOR RETENTION

The Dr Reddy's Story

"They always say time changes
things, but you actually have to
change them yourself."

—Andy Warhol

COMPANY PROFILE

Dr Reddy's Laboratories Ltd (NYSE: RDY) is an integrated global pharmaceutical company, committed to providing affordable and innovative medicines for healthier lives. Through its three businesses—Pharmaceutical Services and Active Ingredients, Global Generics and Proprietary Products—Dr Reddy's offers a portfolio of products and services including Active Pharmaceutical Ingredients, Custom Pharmaceutical Services, Generics, Biosimilars and Differentiated Formulations. Major markets include India, USA, Russia-CIS and Europe apart from other select geographies within Emerging Markets. Dr Reddy's employs over 16,500 people worldwide with twenty-three plus Nationalities. For more information, log on to www.drreddys.com.

CREATING URGENCY AROUND A VISION FOR CHANGE

The McKinsey and Company's report '*India Pharma 2020: Propelling access and acceptance, realising true potential*', predicted that the Indian pharmaceutical market would grow to US $55 billion in 2020 and could grow up to US $70 billion in the same period if aggressive growth strategies were implemented. This re-emphasised the fact that a focus on India was essential to achieve a revenue maximising strategy for both global as well as Indian pharmaceutical companies.

The Indian market for generic pharmaceuticals is a prescription-driven market which means that the doctors are the ones who most often determine product sales. Therefore building and sustaining strategic relationships with medical practitioners is critical for maximising sales revenue for most pharmaceutical companies.

In India, Medical Sales Representatives who are designated as either Medical Representative (MR) or Professional Service Representatives (PSR), periodically visit medical practitioners to appraise them on various products and provide medicine samples to create and sustain a result-oriented PSR-Doctor relationship. A key dimension of this relationship is that some doctors tend to be more loyal towards a Professional Service Representative (PSR) as opposed to a pharmaceutical brand. Therefore any attrition of PSRs has a long term impact on revenues and loss of opportunities which negatively impacts brand equity.

Most pharmaceutical companies undergo a significant cost in recruiting and training their medical representatives. Therefore, attrition of these employees not only leads to immediate loss of revenues and opportunities in an expanding market but posits a significant opportunity cost, given the lead time taken to renew previously existing relationships with medical practitioners. The flipside of reducing the expenditure on training PSRs is potential customer dissonance due to a dichotomy between the practiced and professed values of the organisation, which would adversely impact brand equity.

Dr Reddy's had been experiencing the challenge of 'infant mortality' with new incumbents of their sales force leaving the organisation within three to six months of joining. This was a paradoxical finding given that Dr Reddy's was an aspirational employer brand, provided competitive compensation and had an employee-friendly work environment driven by a high emphasis on ethics. The challenge therefore was to not only control the prevailing attrition rates on a war-footing but to also identify and address the root cause of the problem thereby negating potential loss of revenue/ market share in the medium run.

After much introspection within the HR Community and the Business Units, the diagnosis concluded was that the challenge of 'infant mortality' of Professional Service Representatives (PSRs) could be attributed to a 'not-so-robust' hiring process and the fact that associates who had worked at Dr Reddy's enjoyed a premium in the market. The key challenge therefore was to create a structured and uniform approach for recruitment, across the hiring organisation and to also ensure that the Sales Representatives being recruited had the right functional and behavioural competencies.

To address this, Dr Reddy's decided to introduce Competency based Interviewing to make the Hiring process more robust. This was undertaken to bring about a consistent and standardised understanding of how an interview needed to be conducted and to also ask the right set of questions to identify 'the right fit' for a particular job. In addition to this, the organisation aimed at revamping the On-Boarding process to ensure faster integration and early engagement of the new employees hired.

OPERATIONALISING THE CHANGE

The starting point of any Competency Based Interview is identifying the right set of competencies for a particular role. The interview questions are then aligned to the competency framework so that the behaviours displayed by candidates in previous assignments (past experience) could be used to suitably predict fitment in the role under consideration (future performance).

Dr Reddy's initiated their change efforts by formulating a design for suitable one-day 'Competency Based Interviewing Skills' workshops. Seeking inputs from various stakeholders, the program was designed using Instructional Design Methodologies and was based on the principles of Adult Learning. It was conceptualised as a structured intervention, comprising of eight hours of class room instruction interspersed with hands on exercises, discussions and intensive role-plays.

The workshop conducted by Senior HR Leaders from Dr Reddy's aimed at providing a detailed overview on the basic premise of Competency based interviewing and the elements of a good selection system. This would in turn help participants master the art of extensive probing to get examples of past behaviour to estimate proficiency with regards a particular competency—relevant to the job/role being considered.

The workshop followed a rigorous certification process that involved assessing the participant's ability to transfer the learning from the workshop to the workplace. The certification process had three components with different weights assigned. This included a ten per cent weightage on a knowledge test administered at the end of the workshop, a forty per cent weightage on documentation of three real time interviews conducted by participants within three months of completion of the workshop and a fifty per cent weightage on two mock interviews of forty-five minutes each in the presence of a panel comprising of two senior leaders.

Participants who qualified in all the three components of the certification process were awarded certifications by the Chief of HR.

At the end of the first round of assessments, participants were graded and categorised in Green (Certified with scores of sixty per cent and above), Yellow (scores between 45–59.9 per cent) and Red (less than forty-five per cent). The participants graded in the Yellow zone had to practice more and come back for the certification, while Red zone participants had to undergo a refresher workshop and practice CBI skills before applying for re-certification.

A total of 133 Regional Sales Managers underwent the training between July 2011 and March 2012 of which fifty-five were finally certified.

Hiring laterals in Dr Reddy's is, like any other organisation, spread out over time and geographies. A robust on boarding process for the new hires is the key for their seamless integration into the organisation.

A seven-hour classroom module titled 'Know Your Business' (KYB) was already in place to drive the on boarding process at Dr Reddy's. This classroom module used to be conducted once in two months at Dr Reddy's Leadership Academy in Hyderabad, India. Creating the quorum (of at least fifty new lateral hires) for launching a KYB meant simultaneously disrupting their regular work schedules, longer absence from the work place and the inevitable, direct and indirect costs associated with classroom training programs.

While synchronising all these variables consumed a considerable amount of executive time and effort, the dropout rates from the KYB modules were unacceptably high. Also, in several cases, the time gap between joining and the KYB inputs was more than two months which negated the purpose of the On-Boarding process.

Dr Reddy's addressed these challenges by adopting Technology Assisted Induction. This was a HR Process change management initiative which involved leveraging e-learning solutions to facilitate Self Directed Learning. The entire KYB content was documented into a seven hour e-module burned on a CD which formed a part of the Induction kit of every new lateral hire. The contents of the CD focused on aligning them with the core values of Dr Reddy's as well as help them gain insights on the pharmaceutical industry, history of the organisation, lines of business and key enabling functions.

The academic discipline to peruse the module was ensured through a mandatory online assessment which a new hire had to clear within ninety days of joining Dr Reddy's.

To further beat back the geographical challenge, the Technology Assisted Induction was subsequently rolled out across all English-speaking geographies also.

DESIGNING A COMMUNICATION STRATEGY AND ENSURING SOUND FEEDBACK MECHANISMS

Given the nature of the Change Intervention the objectives of communication strategies were to successfully create the buy-in of Leaders at Dr Reddy's, ensure the line managers understood the management's intent and clearly articulate the manner in which line managers would be required to integrate the inputs obtained from the Competency Based Interview (CBI) workshop with Dr Reddy's hiring agenda.

The Feedback was in built into the design of the CBI (Competency Based Interview) intervention for Regional Sales Managers undergoing the certification process, with inputs provided on competencies displayed as an Interviewer during the role-plays.

MANAGING INITIAL RESISTANCE AND LEVERAGING EARLY WINS

In order to ensure the success of the change intervention at Dr Reddy's the buy-in was secured from the top two levels of the organisational hierarchy—the India Business Unit (BU) Head and the Vertical Heads by the Corporate HR and Business Unit (BU) HR Teams.

Some of the endorsements substantiating the effectiveness of the change interventions are as follows:

"After participating in the workshop, I now evaluate candidates on their recent past performance, along with their actionable and the final outcome. This gives me concrete evidence of past performance, rather than working on assumptions."

—**Kamalesh Kulkarani—Regional Sales Manager—Aqura-SG, Pune**

"Thanks to Competency Based Interviewing skills, I could improve my understanding about the candidate, on his way of functioning. Now, I look for specific examples of past performance and correlate it with our context. I have seen candidates sharing success stories, but the use of 'follow up' questions and 'probing' technique gives me a better understanding of the candidate."

—**Mukesh Gupta, Regional Sales Manager-Hyderabad.**

INSTITUTIONALISING THE CHANGE TO ENSURE IT STUCK

The institutionalization of Competency Based Interviewing was through a two pronged approach—a structured certification process ensuring transfer of learning from the workshop to the workplace and administrative control ensuring that only certified interviewers were eligible to conduct interviews for recruiting Professional Service Representatives.

The success of the technology aided induction was inbuilt as all the benefits of convenience of deploying and utilising the e-learning module, timeliness of induction inputs to the new hires, low cost, surmounting geographical barriers and releasing executive bandwidth came bundled in one single package. The 'Technology Assisted Induction' also passed the acid test as it found ready takers with all relevant stakeholders—Business Unit HR facilitators, top management, senior leaders and of course, the new lateral hires as well their immediate superiors—and, fifty-seven per cent of the target group (mostly in mid and senior management levels) completing the course and clearing the assessment well in time.

IMPACT ON THE ORGANISATION

The change intervention has accrued twin benefits for the Indian Sales Team by helping Regional Sales Managers (RSMs) address the attrition of the field force and at the same time bringing down the infant mortality rate for Professional Service Representatives within six months of their joining. Forty-five per cent of the RSM's in the Green Zone had less than twenty per cent attrition in their territory, substantiating the impact of the change interventions. What makes this change intervention remarkable is the fact that the entire intervention was conceptualised, designed, delivered and managed by internal talent and did not involve external consultants or high implementation costs.

Also it helped reiterate the importance of 'Talent Acquisition' and early 'On-Boarding' as key processes for ensuring early engagement and retention. The Competency Based Interviewing process helped leaders internalise the competency framework which enhanced participation in other key Talent Management programs.

This chapter is based on the entry submitted by Padma Rajeswari Tata
(Sr. Director & Head—Learning & Talent Management, Dr Reddy's Laboratories Ltd.)
and Joel Chandra (Manager—Learning & Development, Dr Reddy's Laboratories Ltd.)
at the Best Change Interventions of Asia Study 2012

What Dr Reddy's did differently to successfully manage and drive change

The Indian market for generic pharmaceuticals being prescription driven, building and sustaining strategic relationships between medical practitioners and Professional Service Representatives is key for realising the revenue maximising strategies of pharmaceutical organisations.

- Faced with the challenge of 'infant mortality' (high attrition rates among newly hired sales representatives) Dr Reddy's decided to implement Competency based interviewing across the organisation to revisit the manner in which their sales representatives were being hired.

- Dr Reddy's formulated a one-day competency based Interviewing Skills workshop as a structured training intervention.

- A rigorous certification process was institutionalised to assess the participant's transfer of learning from the workshop to the workplace. This was followed by ensuring that only Certified Interviewers were eligible to conduct interviews for recruiting professional sales representatives.

- The organisation introduced Technology Assisted Induction for lateral hires to enable seamless integration.

- The Technology Assisted Induction found ready takers with all relevant stakeholders at Dr Reddy's—Business Unit HR facilitators, top management, new lateral hires as well their immediate Managers. What makes this remarkable is the fact that the entire intervention was conceptualised, designed, delivered and managed by internal talent at Dr Reddy's.

Lessons for Change Managers

The Dr Reddy's story presents the following key lessons for Change Managers conceptualising and driving interventions in organisations:

- While addressing the issue of attrition it is key for organisations to conduct a Diagnosis that enables going back to the drawing board/ handling discordant information and acting on what the organisation knows. As illustrated in the Dr Reddy's story, the organisation identified a not-so-robust hiring process as one of the Key factors for their inability to retain their sales staff.

- The intervention was designed and painstakingly executed to address this existing paint point. This is an indication of the organisation's ability to acknowledge what was 'not working' and ACT on fixing it.

- Bringing a science to the Talent Acquisition process and making Leaders understand the relevance of a robust hiring process and its subsequent linkage with the success of the organisation is the real triumph of this story.

- Implementing Technology Assisted Induction is essential to scale up and standardise the Induction process. Particularly when Alignment and Employeeship are key, deploying Technology Assisted Induction to ensure common messaging among all new hires becomes critical.

- Both Interviewing and Induction are often viewed as transactional activities while both processes are important for transforming and creating an aligned organisation. More rigour into who wears the organisation's badge is key. Understanding and aligning to the badge is even more important., Dr Reddy's attempted to do both.

SPREADING WINGS IN THE WINDS OF CHANGE

The GVK Mumbai International Airport Limited Story

"To improve is to change; to be
perfect is to change often"

—Winston Churchill

COMPANY PROFILE

GVK is a leading Indian conglomerate with diversified interests across various sectors including energy, resources, airports, transportation, hospitality and life sciences. It has pioneered various infrastructure projects such as setting up India's first Independent Power Plant (IPP), first six-lane road project and first Brownfield airport (Mumbai) under the Public Private Partnership model.

GVK made its foray into the aviation sector when Mumbai International Airport Pvt. Ltd. (MIAL), a GVK-led consortium, bagged the mandate to operate, manage and develop the country's busiest airport, Chhatrapati Shivaji International Airport (CSIA) in Mumbai. MIAL was awarded the mandate for operating and modernising the Chhatrapati Shivaji International Airport, Mumbai (CSIA) in April 2006.

MIAL is currently implementing a master plan to build an integrated terminal with a vision and framework to modernise this airport as one of the best airports in the world. After modernization, the new integrated Terminal Building referred to as T2 will be able to accommodate forty million passengers per annum (hundred and ten thousand passengers every day).

GVK MUMBAI INTERNATIONAL AIRPORT PVT LTD (MIAL): PREPARING FOR THE CHANGE

MIAL set itself the transformational vision,

"To be one of the world's best airports that consistently delights customers and be the pride of Mumbai."

To achieve this vision, MIAL adopted the following mission statement:

"To own, develop and operate airports that,

- Conform to highest standards of safety and security
- Provide easy to use, efficient and high quality facilities
- Exceed customer expectations
- Reflect the spirit of Mumbai and the culture and heritage of India
- Create value for stakeholders"

The following were identified as MIAL's core values:

- Customer focus: 'expected' to 'exceptional'
- Passion for excellence: the best, always!
- Teamwork: one team, one dream
- Respect: give to get respect
- Performance driven: make it happen!
- Integrity: integral to what we do

Transitioning a government-run airport into a privatised, contemporary enterprise brought with it significant challenges. The employee resistance and protest against the privatization was massive and necessitated planned communication and engagement efforts towards employee motivation and the creation of a participative mindset. Further, effecting a meaningful transition towards the desired vision required focused skill development and cultural evolution with a deep understanding of existing organisation structures and legacy systems

ACTING ON THE NEED FOR CHANGE

With a primary focus on manpower stabilization, detailed Manpower Planning and Talent Sourcing plans were designed and implemented. This process included partnering with Mercer Consulting for understanding AAI (Airports Authority of India) employee costing and defining the AAI absorption strategy. This strategy also included Assessment Centres with Mercer for a thorough evaluation of absorbed employees. Additionally, a detailed Manpower Rationalization Study was conducted with Hewitt Associates post the Operations Support period.

Talent Sourcing was greatly facilitated by the partnership with ACSA (Airports Company South Africa), which lent critical support in manning the Level One Operations organisation through the deployment/ recruitment of expatriates. Additionally national and international search consultants were also partnered with, given the specialised nature of different roles. Campus recruitment was also activated to cater to entry-level talent needs.

During this initial phase, key HR Policies were framed in collaboration with Mercer, with a total of eleven policies being designed and rolled out using best in class and relevant market benchmarks. A comprehensive goal-based Performance Management System was also instated, based on the Balanced Scorecard framework. With these significant developments on the HR Policies and Processes front, an HR Policy Manual was also created for the ready reference of all employees.

With these building blocks in place, i.e. the right people and the required people processes and policies, MIAL set about working towards its transformational vision, confident that this foundation would hold it in good stead for the challenges ahead.

BUILDING URGENCY TOWARDS THE TRANSFORMATIONAL VISION

Embarking on a path-breaking project of operating, managing and developing the country's busiest airport naturally brought with it a sense of urgency towards the required transformation. This was reflected in the Vision, Mission and Values that MIAL adopted.

As part of the privatization agreement with the Government, GVK MIAL was required to quickly upgrade the airport infrastructure and passenger facilities and conform to a host of world class service standards. The scale of these challenges was further magnified by the fact that the airport was one of the most constrained in the world, with land shortage, slum encroachments and ill-planned airside facilities.

The drive towards overcoming these steep challenges was spearheaded by the Leadership in collaboration with HR. Early enough in the game GVK MIAL, led by the Managing Director Mr Sanjay Reddy, brought in a new management team and articulated the transformational vision that envisaged making Mumbai airport 'one of the best airports in the world and the pride of Mumbai'. Through extensive communication and demonstrating a will to succeed against the most difficult odds, the Management Team drove the employees forwards to achieve the impossible.

WORKING TO MAKE THE CHANGE A REALITY

From the very beginning, the importance of evolving and managing the people aspect of the organisation was clear to all concerned. It is for this reason that this massive change intervention was led by HR, albeit with the constant backing and support of the MIAL Leadership. The following were the key steps taken up by HR in this regard:

- Top Level organisation structure firmed up along-with reporting hierarchy in October 2006

- Existing AAI Airport Operations structure was studied and detailed MIAL Operations Structure was created through the active support of ACSA team members in Q1 2007.

- In principle agreement of 'career level' structure for MIAL—linkage to AAI grades from an absorption perspective established in April 2007

- Redefinition of organisation structures post the absorption process and creation of ideal organisation structures for all departments

- Grade, compensation and responsibility matrix for Executive & Bargainable staff defined and implemented

The Senior Team was brought on board through a mechanism of extensive consultation and communication, supported constantly by the Managing Director, Mr Sanjay Reddy. The wisdom of the Leadership Team was reflected in how it set the organisational tone towards facing and overcoming challenges posed by diverse stakeholders, made necessary by the capital and relationship intensive nature of the Infrastructure sector. Thus from the very beginning, the top team was given a directive to never adopt a 'combative attitude' towards any external party, government agency, union or political party and instead maintaining a more solution-focused orientation, seeking the resolution of issues through a constructive, forward-looking process. The top team was given a lot of authority and empowerment to solve problems and ensure sustained momentum towards the adopted transformational vision.

As part of Talent Acquisition, great emphasis was placed on selecting team players. Moreover the HR Team was quick to put in place employee friendly policies and practices important for creating a secure work atmosphere, particularly in the midst of unprecedented change. This also included an effective recognition and rewards system. With these pre-requisites in place, the spirit of challenge and pride came to the fore acting as catalysts for change efforts and adoption.

In order to ensure accountability and ownership, role clarity was ensured through the different phases of change execution and adoption, with clear job descriptions and functional boundaries being defined. Regular team meetings served to reinforce assigned roles, while also allowing for course correction as required with greater transparency and agility.

SEGMENTED COMMUNICATIONS FOR DRIVING CHANGE AND ACTIVE FEEDBACK

Setting the context for the entire project, focused communications were deployed to clarify the multi-faceted benefits that the change would bring not just to MIAL as a whole, but to each member of the organisation. A Mass Contact program titled 'Parivartan' (change) was organised, highlighting key aspects and perspectives regarding the change, covering all employees at the time of transition. 'Drishti-kon' (perspective), the Employee Engagement survey, was deployed covering all employees (1600 plus employees participated including AAI) to keep a pulse on different factors impacting engagement and motivation. Additionally, 'Open House' sessions were held with all Department Heads, and an 'Ice Breaking' dinner organised for all executives. Leveraging recognition as a lever for change, 'MIALite of the Month' was launched to reinforce and role-model desired behaviours and attitudes.

Technology was also leveraged to drive a two-way communication with a dedicated Employee Communication platform being set up on the organisation-wide intranet.

OVERCOMING RESISTANCE AND BUILDING MOMENTUM

As per the terms of MIAL's agreement with the Government, initially it had to keep all erstwhile Government employees on rolls for a period of three years. In view of the hostility of this employee group to the entire privatization effort, GVK MIAL was quick to build up its own team, reducing dependence on the former, while ensuring that the approach was never combative. This conscious, overarching approach helped diffuse many a difficult situation on the path to change.

Being a high profile public utility ensured that there was regular feedback from the three external entities that mattered most—passengers, airlines and the government. The initial changes made at the airport received positive feedback from passengers and other stakeholders, which also helped galvanise efforts and build positive momentum. Additionally, airports being global businesses provide ample opportunities to benchmark with the best in the world. GVK MIAL adopted extensive measurement and benchmarking mechanisms to invigorate and focus energies towards the espoused vision.

Learning & Development was leveraged in a great way in order to drive acceptance and adoption. 'As-is' training analysis was conducted on past training history to identify deficiencies in different areas and possible measures to address the same. Learning Trips were conducted to various International Airports for almost all employees. 110 Executives were taken through Mercer's miLEAP Workshop, culminating in the identification of relevant developmental areas. Additionally, structured learning sessions (LEAD—Learn, Enrich, Align & Deploy) were conducted on various behavioural and functional subject areas.

Managing and taking the unions on board with respect to key aspects of the change was another important step in overcoming initial resistance. All pending labour disputes were analyzed and closely worked upon with the Legal Cell. Additionally, efforts were invested towards relationship building with HR counterparts from Airports Authority of India (AAI) and labour regulatory authorities as well.

INSTITUTIONALISING THE CHANGE TO ENSURE IT STICKS

Both the Leadership and HR at GVK MIAL were aware of the need to institutionalise desired changes for the achievement of the transformational vision, becoming 'one of the best airports in the world and the pride of Mumbai'. As a result, rigorous follow-up and active senior leadership participation were sustained at every stage of the process.

The deployment of new HR systems, such as Balanced Scorecard cascade, online Performance Management and Leave Management with Biometric Attendance among others, helped cement the change further. Additionally, a detailed Leadership System was designed and deployed to equip leaders to effectively lead the enterprise towards its vision.

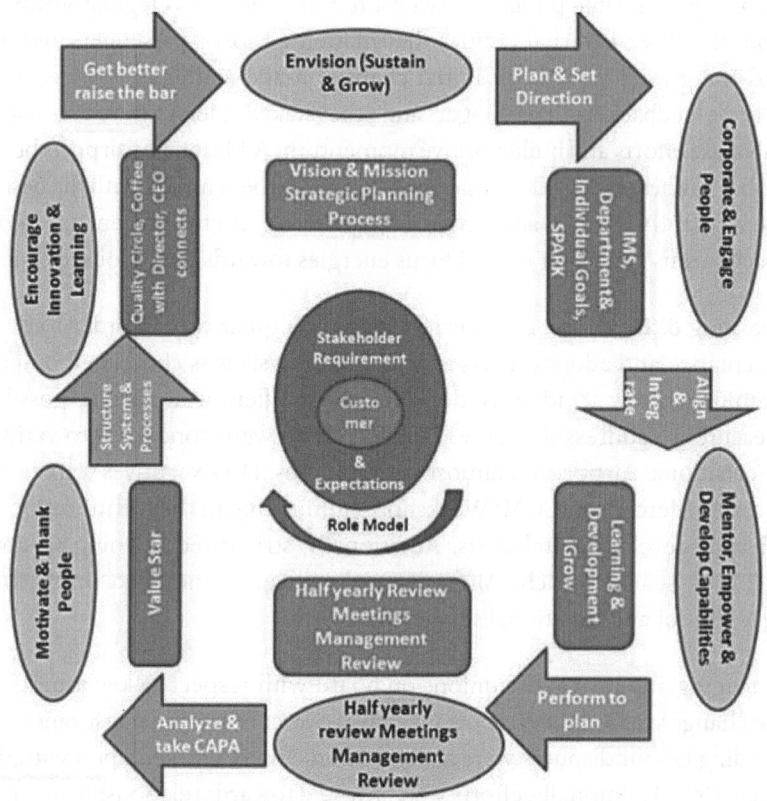

MIAL Leadership System (LS)

The Vision, Mission & Values (VMV) are deployed through MIAL's Leadership System (LS) at all levels. The light blue boxes are roles that cannot be delegated. The violet arrows articulate key activities of the leadership. The orange boxes are key approaches of MIAL that facilitate organisational delivery on its Vision, Mission and Values. This Leadership

System is reviewed by CEOs and HODs during different Review and Planning meets through the year and across functions.

Sustaining Change with a culture of Continuous Process Improvement

Transitioning from a government-run body to a lean, privatised, world-class entity, GVK MIAL was aware of the synergies that a Continuous Improvement program could lend to driving sustainable change. With this keen insight in mind, MIAL was certified to a series of management system standards including ISO9001:2008 (Quality Management System), ISO10002:2004 (Complaint Management System) and ISO14001:2004 (Environment Management System) among others.

> "The most important impact of this change on business was the improvement in turnaround time. The buffer time between an aircraft vacating a bay and another entering the bay which used to be forty-five minutes has now reduced to fifteen minutes. This has helped in better utilization of the parking bays."
>
> —Manoj Rajimwale (Vice President HR, GVK-MIAL)

The drive towards continuous improvement was further strengthened with the launch of SPARK, the Employee Suggestion Scheme aimed at providing an opportunity for employees to communicate ideas, promote participation and imbibe the spirit of co-operation and teamwork and VALUE STAR, the Employee Recognition Scheme designed to appreciate MIALites for putting in their best efforts in the pursuit of excellence.

IMPACT ACHIEVED

A major benefit the organisation accrued from the rigorous change efforts was the strengthening of HR capabilities and processes, which form the foundation for successful change delivery.

Robust Talent Acquisition Process—Hire the Best!

Rapid technological changes, escalating labour costs, shifting job requirements, rising education and expectation levels among employees and high performance levels demanded by increasing competition—all have

Human Capital Strategy Model – REACH
It's about reaching the goal together

- Recognize – We recognize the potential in you
- Empower - We empower you with opportunities o showcase your potential
- Align – We enable alignment between your efforts and the overall business strategy of the organization
- Care – We care about your professional environment and personal well-being
- Honour – We honour your efforts through different Reward mechanisms

contributed to the need for manning an organisation with both suitable and competent manpower. The objective of the recruitment process at GVK—MIAL is to provide a sufficiently large group of qualified and competent candidates to cater to the needs of organisation.

Effective Talent Management and Retention

GVK MIAL works with an astute awareness of the fact that people are its greatest strength and asset. There is a need felt to develop knowledge, skills and perspectives on a continuous basis to harness the innovative and differentiated talent of the workforce. Employee learning and development is therefore an integral part of the MIAL Human Resource Philosophy.

Continuous Improvement with Industry Benchmark Surveys

As part of the annual employee satisfaction survey, MIAL participates in the Great Place To Work® Survey to ascertain feedback/evaluation of its people practices and benchmark the same across the industry. Apart from this, MIAL also participates in various surveys on Compensation, Workforce Planning and others to continue to benchmark with the best and keep the momentum of its change journey, remaining focused on its vision of change.

This chapter is based on the entry submitted by Manoj Rajimwale (Vice President—HR, GVK—Mumbai International Airport Pvt. Ltd) at the Best Change Interventions of Asia Study 2012

What GVK MIAL did differently to successfully manage and drive change

GVK MIAL managed to overcome towering odds to achieve its vision of making Mumbai airport 'one of the best in the world and the pride of Mumbai'. The following were some of the highlights of this change effort:

- The multi-pronged communications deployed by GVK MIAL ensured all employee segments were covered and influenced towards accepting and internalising the change.

- Driving continuous improvement while institutionalising the desired change was a very positive step taken by GVK MIAL, given how the former lends itself synergistically to the context of acknowledging, accepting and adopting change.

- Actively engaging with and aligning unions the way GVK MIAL did, was no easy feat. This challenge was further accentuated by the fact that the organisation was inheriting a legacy system and environment that was essentially government-run and union dominated.

Lessons for Change Managers

The GVK MIAL story presents several valuable lessons for Change Managers:

- The articulation, adoption and active communication of a truly transformational vision can help galvanise efforts and build positive momentum for the change, as was evident in the case of GVK MIAL.

- Given the context and environment in which MIAL set about developing the airport, it was clear that people and people processes would form a vital aspect of the change intervention. Thus it was clear that HR would lead the change backed unstintingly by the leadership team. Identifying which function/ team should lead the change agenda, depending on vital organisational needs, is key.

- Once leaders are onboard and backing the change agenda, it is not uncommon for change managers to focus their energies exclusively on the rest of the organisation. However, it is important to keep a pulse on how enabled and equipped the leaders themselves are to drive the change as required. Supporting them with an awareness of the different needs posed at different stages of the change effort is essential for their sustained involvement and participation.

THROUGH THE PRISM OF CHANGE

The HMEL Story

"Change is the law of life and those who look only to the past or present are certain to miss the future."

—John F. Kennedy

COMPANY PROFILE

HPCL-Mittal Energy Limited (HMEL) is a joint venture between Hindustan Petroleum Corporation Limited (HPCL) and Mittal Energy Investment Pte Ltd, Singapore— a Lakshmi N Mittal Group Company. This landmark public-private partnership company has built the 9 MMTPA Guru Gobind Singh Refinery at Bhatinda, Punjab.

HMEL—IN A STATE OF INCEPTION

HMEL is a Greenfield refinery operating in a highly volatile global energy market that forces refining companies to cut operational costs and respond with agility and accuracy in decision making. This drive towards business results is governed by six core Values:

Safety First	Achieve Targets and Meet Deadlines	High Ethical Standards
Respect for People	Continuous Improvement and Learning	Teamwork

Early in the game, the overarching objective of the organisation was to run HMEL as a 'World-class Organisation'. In this regard, Cost Competitiveness, World Class Processes, Agility and Quick Decision making and a Talented and Experienced Workforce were identified as Critical Success Factors.

With this unique Public—Private joint venture bringing together contrasting cultures, perspectives and working styles, the need for a common, world-class set of systems and processes was evident; and thus was born, Project Prism.

Project Prism @ HMEL

The vision of Project Prism was to sustain 'World-class business processes and cutting edge business applications' to enable integration of the 'Shop-floor' (field instrumentation) with the 'Top-floor' (Management Dashboards). Project Prism was conceived to facilitate the design, implementation and management of business processes and IT applications at HMEL, in sync with the commissioning of the refinery itself. The Project brought the HMEL employees and implementation partners together to form a strong team which helped HMEL in adopting world-class processes and systems in Operating and Maintaining the HMEL Refinery and Pipeline System. Impacting an employee base of over 1,000, Project Prism was planned to include:

- Implementation of key processes in the Refinery value stream
- SAP ERP implementation covering fourteen modules
- Designing and implementing Manufacturing Execution Systems (MES) covering over sixteen Refinery applications; the Manufacturing Excellence Systems(MES) was then to be integrated with SAP

The functional and technical integration aimed by this project was extremely complex and crucial for the achievement of business results. With this in mind, HMEL designed its organisation structure in a manner that functionally supported the integration. IBM was engaged for the design, implementation and integration of the MES and Enterprise Performance Management System. While Prism Team worked together with business users and IT experts to achieve technical integration, the HR and Change team focused on functional integration of the organisation. Project Prism was naturally a key agenda from an HR and culture building perspective as well. With employees from over 140 different companies coming together in the organisation, it was clear that this project would significantly shape the desired HMEL Culture, preparing the organisation to deliver on business goals.

CREATING URGENCY AROUND THE PROJECT PRISM VISION

Project Prism was conceived as the umbrella program for implementing business applications at HMEL. Owing to the unique organisational context, it faced some unique challenges on this front. Employees coming in from different organisations (as many as 140) and backgrounds, came in drawing on diverse cultures and work ethics, most of which were contrary to the high collaboration and empowerment energies espoused by Project Prism. With system implementation being targeted to coincide with refinery commissioning, the team had a very short timeframe for adoption. These challenges were further accentuated by the fact that several key employees were yet to be hired.

In view of these factors, it was clear that sound change management with active sponsorship from leaders was the need of the hour. Therefore, the first person to adopt this vision for change was the CEO & Managing Director, Mr Prabh Das himself, who was the Project Sponsor, with the Chief Financial Officer (CFO) and Chief Commercial Officer (CCO) being co-sponsors. All Business Heads formed part of the Steering Committee. This helped create sense of urgency, flowing from the top management levels. The core HMEL values, articulated by the Leadership Team within months of the organisation's inception, were deployed as vehicles for driving and institutionalising the change agenda.

The program was actively branded to enhance connect and recall among employees. The title 'Project Prism' was finalised after an internal competition, thus enhancing participation from the very beginning. Multiple channels were activated to obtain continuous feedback and keep a pulse on the organisation's receptivity and progress towards the change. This included Engagement Surveys, Culture and Change Readiness Diagnostics among others.

MAKING PROJECT PRISM A REALITY

The gap between planning and implementation is often the difference between successful, high impact change interventions and those that crash with a whimper after the launch itself. With this awareness, efforts were made towards the effective deployment of Project Prism, before, during and after design and implementation. The change program was focused on three different aspects of execution—to ensure that all key interventions were deployed as per plan, to take roadblocks and setbacks in its stride as lessons learned and battles won, and to be open and flexible to anticipate, accept and incorporate any adjustments required mid-course. Changes to the program were mainly results of feedback received from readiness surveys and other inputs from the various stakeholder groups via multiple channels. Change readiness surveys were conducted to measure the awareness of users and their readiness for adoption of the processes and systems comprising Project Prism. These surveys helped identify key risks and issues to be addressed with appropriate measures. The second survey measured the effectiveness of these initiatives and checked whether the program was proceeding meaningfully on the path to successful implementation. Additionally, change management was not a separate track but rather a part of the Program Management Office itself. This enhanced leadership buy-in and ensured visibility on key people & organisation issues. It also helped in the commitment of requisite investments for a successful change management.

Project Prism was unique in the way it was conceived ; as being organisation and people focused rather than stressing purely on process and technology. This was evident from how the stakeholders from across the organisation were engaged in the change process through Prism Roadshows, Design Workshops, SAP & MES Overview sessions and Stakeholder Connect sessions. A unique initiative started by the COO, fondly called 'Samosa (Indian Snack) Party', entailed a monthly quiz based on a chosen topic/ theme with top-scoring employees winning prizes. This was an instant hit as it created awareness on the key change areas and ensured participation across departments.

With HMEL offices spread across the country, it was important to have people at these locations connected and in sync with the change agenda. A network of change champions called the 'Core Team' was formed across the organisation to play the crucial role of early adopters and influencers, role-modelling and championing different aspects of the project, disseminating information to employees and providing support to handhold users through the change. Later this network was extended for post-Go Live support as the 'Super User Network'.

HMEL used the change implementation strategy advocated by the time tested 'Change Diamond' (from IBM) to identify the key ingredients for a successful change intervention and embedded these into the Project

Prism change strategy. It identifies four key ingredients for driving successful change viz., Real insights, Solid methods, Better Skills and Right Investments.

INTELLIGENT COMMUNICATIONS TO TAKE PROJECT PRISM TO THE MASSES

In-depth communication and feedback mechanisms formed important cogs of the Change Management efforts. The Prism Team worked together on this, to ensure minimal lag between insight and action. The communication strategy was designed to address the needs of employees across levels and from different business units and also to ensure streamlining to avoid messages getting lost in clutter or in translation. Findings from the Readiness surveys were fed back in to fine tune the strategy; for instance surveys revealed that employees preferred the e-mail and visual media most—the former owing to accessibility over smart devices and the latter to enhanced recall and appeal (resulting in mass poster campaigns for all elements of Project Prism).

In order to maximise coverage and efficacy of communication, existing communication channels (such as the monthly newsletter 'Expressions') were utilised along with new ones—such as the Prism Intranet Portal. Key milestones and success stories of the adoption in different departments were publicised and celebrated, fostering a healthy competition across the organisation.

HMEL being a Greenfield organization was ramping up in phases to ensure the right talent was on-boarded at the right time. This posed a huge challenge to Project Prism's training program as it had to be highly flexible to meet the varied training needs of different departments. Additionally, compressed timelines and competing priorities with ongoing refinery construction and commissioning added to the challenges faced by training efforts. To overcome these challenges an innovative training strategy was devised wherein a Big Bang classroom training was conducted for all users one month before go-live, followed by Self-directed learning avenues. Over 13,000 man-hours of training were delivered in multiple rounds to over 800 employees across HMEL, covering all locations with an average training rating of 4.4 on a scale one to five (five being 'Best') and an average attendance of seventy per cent, in spite of conflicting and strict refinery commissioning schedules.

BUILDING MOMENTUM FOR ADOPTION

Given that HMEL was still in its infancy stage as an organisation when Project Prism took off, it did not suffer from the common challenges of contending with established legacy systems and turning around employee perspectives thereof. However, its unique position with employees having joined from over 140 different companies meant there were natural pockets of resistance arose across departments and locations. These manifested themselves in minimal attendance in training sessions, deviations on milestone timelines and even low system usage post go-live. These were countered by announcing department-wise adoption data to all managers, creating pressure on department heads and managers to influence participation.

Directed leadership communications were launched stressing on the importance of training and orientation sessions in the context of the larger change agenda. Dedicated contact sessions were held with lagging departments/ groups to understand problems related to system usage and adoption.

HMEL also instituted a core value award for employees demonstrating one or more of the core values in their day-to-day activities. This was a great way of encouraging employees to achieve the organisational goals and build a high performance culture. In addition to this Project Prism also instituted 'Star of the Month' award where the top contributors for the month were recognised and rewarded.

Additionally, the presence of senior leaders in the Project Steering Committee, along with sponsorship from Mr Prabh Das (MD & CEO—HMEL), the CFO and COO helped resolve issues in a timely and effective manner without impacting project timelines. Early wins were recognised and celebrated across the project implementation departments, leading to a closer connect between the Project team and end users departments. The resulting camaraderie and momentum helped further expedite subsequent process steps.

INTEGRATING PROJECT PRISM INTO THE HMEL WAY OF WORKING

The change program at HMEL created a strong foundation towards achieving its goal of becoming a world-class refinery. But it was felt, and rightfully so, that more dedicated efforts were required to ensure that the change stuck and became an integral part of the organisation's DNA. As a result, immediately after the completion of the project implementation, a sustenance plan was created to support and hand-hold users. This was done to ensure the momentum gained during change efforts was not lost.

All dual pathways and legacy systems were discontinued post go-live to pre-empt the natural human tendency of reverting to the status quo. This was complemented with regular feedback mechanisms ,course corrections and improvements as identified across departments/ processes. Necessary changes were made to systems and processes which increased the user acceptance and adoption of systems and processes.

In addition to this, HMEL continued to drive ownership, reinforce leadership commitment, and provide on-going process support to maintain and enhance system usage as well as user confidence.

PROJECT PRISM IMPACT

Project Prism impacted over 1,000 HMEL employees across various levels and had a significant impact on people and the organisation at large. The program ensured that the processes and systems were embedded into the HMEL DNA, with employees making it a part of their way of life.

Project Prism positively impacted the way employees and other stakeholders carry out work activities and benefit from the organisation, with employees now more empowered through the Employee Self Service Portal and more productive with collaborative features on the intranet portal. It also facilitated greater transparency of processes and systems enabling the employees to function without fear or favour.

> "Project Prism has brought in transparency to the business by bringing in clarity of process and practices in everything done at HMEL. It has improved the collaboration among the employees by ensuring various parts of the HMEL work with each other in a synchronized manner delivering higher value for HMEL."
>
> —Harak Banthia, CFO—HMEL

Project Prism created a significant operational impact by improving efficiency and optimising of the value chain. Accurate and timely oil stock accounting without manual intervention was made possible by integration between Honeywell Materials Movement Application and SAP. Collaborative Telecom Facilities (Using Blackberry and Smart Phones) enabled employees to stay connected on the move. Environment, Health and Safety Modules of SAP helped track environmental compliance, health and hygiene parameters and safety compliance. These and other operational improvements resulted in significant financial benefits for the organisation.

From a strategic viewpoint, Project PRISM enabled HMEL in building a lean, efficient and process driven organisation. This has helped the organisation gain a competitive edge in the Oil and Gas industry, with a comprehensive integration of various Business Applications aimed at transactional efficiency with stringent controls and checks. The various modules of the system also resulted in improved collaboration among employees, partners and customers.

This chapter is based on the entry submitted by Ashok Kumar (Vice President—HR, HPCL Mittal Energy Ltd.) and Girish H (Head—Organisation Development, HPCL Mittal Energy Ltd.) at the Best Change Interventions of Asia Study 2012

What HMEL did differently to successfully manage and drive change

HMEL presents a unique story with several valuable take-aways, given how a Greenfield project with employees from over 140 organisations converging together managed to successfully drive change at multiple levels, at the time of its very inception:

- Among the many things that HMEL got right, right in the beginning, was the decision to house the entire change effort in the Project Management Office itself, with timelines in sync with the refinery commissioning. This was key as the very existence of the Greenfield project hinged on the successful management of change.

- Given that HMEL was effectively a new entity by itself, the Management was quick to identify the core values that would define work and life within the organisation. These values were then deployed as the fundamental vehicles for change, as an integral part of the envisioned future.

- The active involvement of the Executive Leadership in different aspects of the change efforts helped reinforce the importance of the initiative among all stakeholders; this was particularly important in view of the massive heterogeneity of the employee base.

Lessons for Change Managers

The HMEL story brings to the fore important lessons in the area of managing and driving change:

- The partnership with the engaged solutions provider must not be restricted to a limited definition of the service. Rather, an in-depth understanding of the organisational needs must lead to an more integrated approach to the partnership, as HMEL did when driving change through the IBM Change Diamond approach.

- A very practical lesson to be learnt from HMEL is how all alternative pathways and legacy systems were shut out once the new system was launched. This ensures that the natural tendency to retreat to status quo is curtailed, while also necessitating a level of rigour and completeness in the change efforts preceding it.

- HMEL used peer pressure and a sense of competition to ease out the initial resistance. This is a prime example of diverting focus from the intimidating idea of change and uncertainty and stressing instead on the desired results.

ABHILASHA— AN ARDENT DESIRE TO CHANGE

The Lafarge Story

"The only way to make sense out of change is to plunge into it, move with it, and join the dance."

—Alan Watts

COMPANY PROFILE

A world leader in building materials, Lafarge employs 65,000 people in sixty-four countries and has posted sales of € 15.8 billion (21.16 billion USD) in 2012. As a top-ranking player in Cement, Aggregates and Concrete businesses, it contributes to the construction of cities around the world through its innovative solutions, providing them with more· housing and making them more compact, durable, beautiful and better connected. With the world's leading building materials research facility, Lafarge places innovation at the heart of its priorities in order to contribute to more sustainable construction and serve architectural creativity.

Since 2010, the Lafarge Group has been a part of the Dow Jones Sustainability World Index, the first Global Sustainability benchmark, in recognition of its sustainable development actions.

The Context for Change

Lafarge India acquired Larsen & Toubro's concrete business in 2008, inheriting over eighty plants across the country and leadership position in the market. Subsequently, other ready mix players started expanding their presence & market share. Commercial Ready Mix forms twenty per cent of the total market of the 100 million cubic meters. The Ready Mix Business has changed drastically in the recent past, with competition from local as well as organised players putting tremendous pressure on the market. Customer needs had changed and so had their expectations. Though the market was stagnating with only marginal business growth, the new leadership team saw opportunities in evolving customer needs and

Lafarge's ability to offer innovative products. However, quick action was needed if the business was to capitalise on the opportunities.

The need of the hour was to revamp the business and bring in a turnaround by focusing on shifting the following levers:

- Shifting focus from merely low price bidding to Prescriptive selling, increasing volume and delivering Value Added Products.

- Building efficiencies in core operational areas like plant utilization, delivery schedules, transit mixers and pumps maintenance, raw material quality & cost.

- Market mapping and strategically improving customer base.

- Building passionate and motivated teams with clear direction around the turnaround plan which would allow Lafarge to attract and retain skilled professionals for long term success.

To realise this turnaround, the Ready Mix India leadership team worked intensively on defining the changes necessary for capitalising on the opportunities available in the market. This initiative was aptly named *'Abhilasha 2015'* which means **Desire** reflecting the ardent desire of the team to change.

CREATING URGENCY AROUND A VISION FOR CHANGE

With *'Abhilasha 2015'*, Lafarge Ready Mix had an ambition to emerge as the safest, most reliable and preferred Business Partner for the construction industry, which would be achieved by providing high quality products, consistent reliable services, and innovative solutions, delivered by high performing teams.

'Abhilasha 2015' identified customer focus and adaptability to a fast changing external environment as two important dimensions of the change required to achieve this ambition. People were at the heart of this initiative and hence the emphasis was on empowering and enhancing people development.

> "The primary agenda of *Abhilasha* 2015 was to make Lafarge RMX the safest, most reliable and preferred business partner for the construction industry in India. This will be achieved by providing high quality products, consistent reliable services, innovative solutions, with the support of our Lafarge employees."
>
> —Frederic Guimbal, MD—Ready-Mix Concrete, Lafarge India

To ensure a sense of urgency, challenging timelines were drawn up for all actions with Sponsors and Leaders identified to drive the program through periodic reviews.

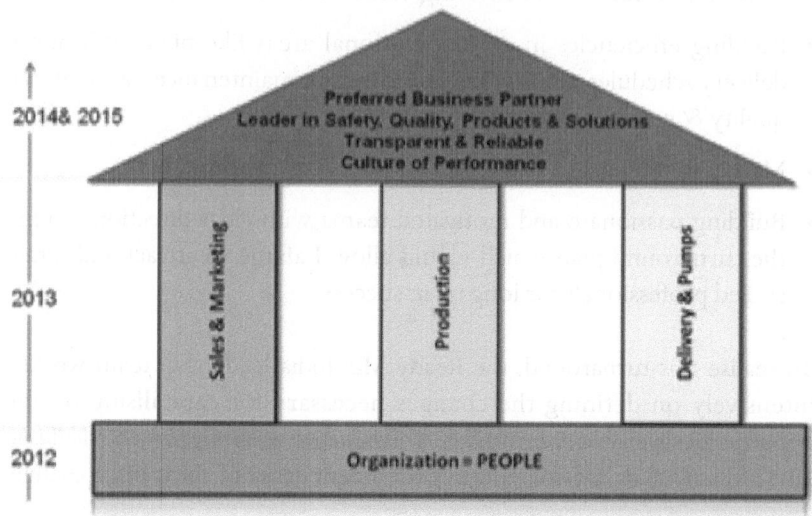

VISION and how to get there

Organisation = People	Sales & Marketing
<ul><li>Finalization of new Organisational Structure—Job Descriptions & Competency assessment for critical positions</li><li>Infusing fresh energy(Recruitment through external consultants) and job rotation for critical positions</li><li>Develop customer centricity among employees through training like Sales Force effectiveness and Operational training like Quality Circles</li><li>Constant communication of milestones achieved</li></ul>	<ul><li>Market segmentation of Customer base</li><li>Pricing Model created and clear delegation of tasks and authority</li><li>Focus on prescriptive selling</li><li>Development of Sales KPI with focused utilization of Market intelligence</li></ul>

Production	Delivery & Pumps
• Development of Standard Operating Procedures • Plant Network Optimization through definition of clusters, upgradation of existing plants and setting up new plants • Development of Performance KPIs • Continued focus on Quality	• Development of Standard Operating Procedures specifically for scheduling and delivery • Task force comprising of Marketing & Procurement Team formed to develop sourcing best practices, Safety & housekeeping • Development of Delivery Performance KPIs

OPERATIONALISING CHANGE

All the key influencers and senior leadership members were involved in the strategy design from the beginning. Each functional head worked on his/ her respective functional SWOT, identified industry benchmarks and key opportunities and weaknesses that needed to be addressed. The entire management team together reviewed each proposal and finally selected five key focus areas.

A business proposal was prepared with projections over five years, highlighting cost benefit analysis of working on the identified areas. The plan clearly required additional investments in the initial years with returns expected from the third year onwards.

It was a great moment of accomplishment for the entire team when the proposal was approved by the Lafarge Management. The proposal focussed on long term benefits, market penetration to create a niche in promising developing markets.

Following actionables were identified to operationalise this turnaround plan:

1. **A new organisational structure was proposed to enhance consumer connect and effectiveness with the following features:**

   • Creation of new positions for effectively managing three to four plants in major markets

- Training of Sales Managers for prescriptive selling for every plant
- Additional Sales Managers in larger markets
- Strengthening the Quality function with the creation of an Area Quality Manager position
- Well trained workforce with focus on Sales Force Effectiveness, Value Selling and Technical Selling
- Separate Maintenance and Safety function at area level
- Updating of relevant job descriptions

2. **Table Stakes—Upgrade Quality and Lafarge Brand Equity:**

- Transit Mixers & Plant Silos painting and maintenance were upgraded to reflect the international Lafarge brand
- Quality linked failures were to be tracked and made part of Key Performance Indicators (KPIs) throughout the organisation
- Aggregates & Cement was to ensure procurement of consistent quality of raw material

3. **Segment based Sales and Marketing**

- A detailed segment based marketing plan and branding architecture was created to support turnaround strategy
- Clearly articulated selling approach for different segments, i.e. 'basic offer', Value Added Products and Key Account Management projects were developed
- Efforts were focussed on Prescriptive Selling through Construction Business System specialists and Key Account Managers. 'Value selling toolkits' were also created for each value added product
- Efforts were focussed on services and application
- Efforts were extended to small customers through revised KPIs

4. **A Detailed plan was developed for capacity expansion on some existing plants, new plants and plant movements within and across cities**

5. **Restructuring of Key Account Management/Projects team with Projects Head reporting into the CEO**

- Project teams were created to provide offers with a One Lafarge mindset

- Efforts were made to professionalise functions of Project Acquisition, Contracting and Project Execution

After the exciting phase of getting approval on the overall change strategy, the next challenging part was creating a shared vision across levels and implementing this effectively.

The services of an External Project Consultant were hired to assist in the turnaround, supported by a dedicated internal Project team and a Coordinator. The critical mass for successful change adoption was identified as employees' up to middle management level. The task was to involve and drive change through 150 plus managers across the business.

A Large Scale Interactive Process (LSIP) was used to focus on Planning and Execution of change in a large system over a short period of time.

The LSIP methodology was driven by involvement of people and required the Internal Design team to work closely with consultants on the program content and delivery. The design team comprised of cross hierarchical, cross functional representation of the larger team who designed and they delivered a successful LSIP workshop. They not only provided the relevant data but also served as a reality check in making the design more practical and effective in the organisational context. The rationale behind LSIP was to involve and influence employees to believe in the need for change and to ensure the buy-in that precedes adoption.

The whole process began with the Senior Leadership team sharing relevant information about the current scenario like market reality, performance details, customer feedback etc. Employees across the businesses were exposed to information from other key stakeholders. A positive dissatisfaction between 'what is' and 'what can be' was created (Mad, Glad & Sad Exercise). This was followed by multiple level dialogues across levels and functions. These cross location / cross functional and cross hierarchy teams worked on identifying key problems and generating the right solutions. The same was shared with management teams and integrated into the change strategy.

Teams were also given an opportunity to identify and ask questions around the proposed change strategy, which were answered by the Senior Leadership Team.

The Change Managers built momentum through two-day workshops to enable shifts in mindset through common ground and critical mass. The workshop ended with each member and each function head charting out action plans for the next 100 days.

DESIGNING A COMMUNICATION STRATEGY AND ENSURING SOUND FEEDBACK MECHANISMS

A motivational communication plan across various levels of the organisation was rolled out to share the vision and lay down clear expectations and new ways of working. A two day event was designed to develop the road plan for this turnaround plan. Some of the initial teasers can be seen below:

A video was created detailing the current market capitalization, customer service index and customer insights. Since the focus was on shifting the organisation from being 'one among the players' to a differentiated value

BELIEVE WE CAN

TEAMWORK
Togetherness creates winning teams

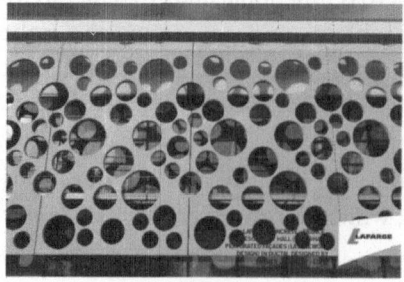

adding solutions provider, there was a strong focus on building Sales Force effectiveness. A program on this theme was designed and deployed to address this.

A detailed communication on LSIP workshops was sent out from the desk of Product Line General Manager to all employees. To ensure alignment and uniform understanding, area level meetings were conducted by Managers who attended LSIP workshops for their respective teams.

MANAGING INITIAL RESISTANCE AND LEVERAGING EARLY WINS TO BUILD MOMENTUM

The LSIP (Large Scale Interactive Process), which focussed on gaining buy-in for the change, was successful in overcoming many of the limitations inherent in traditional approaches to change.

The achievements of the LSIP were:

- Creating a shared vision
- Effective communication of strategy to middle level managers
- Strategy implementation support

Subsequent communication strategy and sharing of success stories helped in keeping the momentum up. The senior leadership team continued working with Managers on the 100 day action plans identified.

INSTITUTIONALISING THE CHANGE

As stated before, a 100-day action planning commitment was charted out by each individual team member, focusing on action plan details with an assurance to complete stated milestones within thirty days, sixty days or 100 days. This was periodically tracked and reviewed. A sample action plan is shown below:

Steering committees were formed to review the various Action Plans and monitor them. Customer Service Centres were formed at all Zonal Offices

abhilasha 2015

LAFARGE

Signature: _Camilla + B_

Action Plan commitment : Individual

Name: _Camill + Zarin_   Function/ Area Name: _Corporate Communication_

Action Plan Details	Comitted timelines for closure		
	30 Days	60 Days	100 Days
1. Abhilasha : thought of the week videos on U Tube			
2. Create Abhilasha platform to style channel			
3. Success stories - learning from experience sharing (newsletters)			
4. Coffee with ccoo + mcm			
5. Monthly 'ask your questions' mailer solutions to be provided			
6. Use FTP for sharing inform			
7. Reporting internally : group to samvaad varta			
8. SEO + microsite			
9. Training and Support HR			

with Tele-callers deployed with the purpose of obtaining honest feedback from customers.

Monthly flash of success stories with recognition from Product Line General Manager were shared with everyone. A sample is provided below:

IMPACT ON THE ORGANISATION

Managers who attended the Large Scale Interactive Process and workshops were able to cascade the philosophy of *Abhilasha* (Desire) down the line. Focused communications were carried out for the larger group of employees through mailers and sharing experiential learning. The immediate change was visible in the energy levels in the actions towards the achievement of *Abhilasha* 100 day plan by all functions. There was a seamless implementation of the new structure across zones and opportunities were provided to internal employees for growth. An additional 185 employees were hired to support these new structures and strengthen the sales and marketing initiatives. With consistent efforts on Sales Force Effectiveness training, the Team has been able to move the needle on increasing Value Added

Production sales, change customer segmentation. The overall customer satisfaction scores have been more than ninety per cent with highest rating for the quality of the product. Transit mixers maintenance and housekeeping at the plants in particular have also witnessed great improvements.

This chapter is based on the entry submitted by Aparna Sharma (Country Head— HR, Lafarge India Pvt. Ltd) at the Best Change Interventions of Asia Study 2012

What Lafarge did differently to successfully manage and drive change

With the objective of capturing the ready mix market in India, Lafarge initiated 'Project *Abhilasha* 2015'. With *Abhilasha*, the organisation wanted to emerge as the safest and most preferred Business Partner in the construction industry by providing high quality products, consistently reliable services and innovative solutions generated by high performing teams.

- A new organisational structure was introduced with the objective of achieving enhanced customer focus and greater productivity of the existing workforce. Cluster Managers were appointed to manage plants in major markets, the quality function was strengthened through creation of Area Quality Managers.

- Sales Managers were trained on 'Sales Force Effectiveness' , 'Value Selling' and 'Technical Selling' to enhance commercial acumen and customer focus.

- The Sales Team were restructured and the Key Account Managers were made to report directly to the CEO to foster greater accountability and quicker decision making.

- Quality linked failures were periodically tracked and made part of the Key Performance Indicators across the organisation.

- A detailed segment based marketing plan and branding architecture was adopted to support the turn-around strategy with an enhanced focus on prescriptive selling and provision of value added products.

- A Large Scale Interactive Process (LSIP) was initiated to drive change and adoption across the organisation. Leaders periodically communicated organisational goals and strategic imperatives to employees ensuring alignment and focus on achieving set performance goals.

- Cross functional teams were created to generate solutions to key organisational pain points, these were periodically shared with the Management Teams and integrated into the change strategy.

- Lafarge built and sustained the momentum of the Change Intervention through the LSIP workshops which ended with each Function Head identifying action plans for the next 100 days with milestones and strict timelines. This helped create a shared vision among employees and supported the implementation of organisational strategy by aligning employees with the organisational goals.

- Success stories were shared across the organisation creating a Best Practices and Lessons Learnt Culture across the organisation.

Lessons for Change Managers

The Lafarge story presents the following lessons for Change Managers:

- The organisation identified a key market segment which had the potential of emerging as a strategic differentiator in terms of enhanced revenue and profits in the medium to long run. Accordingly it launched an organisation wide change intervention with the objective of aligning larger organisational goals with performance goals of individual employees. Lafarge therefore acted on what it knew and implemented a series of directed steps to achieve its goals—a differentiating feature of Learning Organisations across the globe.

- Ensuring alignment and high engagement levels during implementation of the Change Intervention is key. Leaders play a very important role in communicating organisational strategies and short/medium term implications of implemented decisions across employees. This therefore creates an incubating culture which helps manage discordant information.

- To ensure a sense of urgency and maintain momentum, it is imperative that Change Managers create a robust Strategy Articulation document with strict timelines and well-articulated goals. This was a key differentiating feature of *Abhilasha* 2015 which greatly contributed to the success of the change intervention.

- Providing customised learning solutions basis business needs is essential to bridge observed technical, functional and behavioural gaps. Understanding business needs, supporting knowledge transfer post workshops and documenting improvements and sharing success stories is key to ensuring optimal Learning Transfer and change.

DRIVING CULTURAL TRANSFOR- MATION:

A Holistic Approach

The Mahindra Rise Story

"The only way to make sense out of change is to plunge into it, move with it, and join the dance."

—Alan Watts

Mahindra
Rise.

COMPANY PROFILE

Founded in 1945 as a Steel Trading Company, the Mahindra Group has over the years diversified into a number of businesses operating in sectors like Aerospace, Agribusiness, Automotive, Construction equipment, Defence, Energy, Consulting Services, Finance, Hospitality, and Logistics among others. Mahindra's federal structure enables each of its businesses to function independently yet leverage synergies across the entire Group's competencies. A respected global employer, Mahindra operates in over 100 countries and employs over 1,55,000 people globally.

CREATING URGENCY

> "The group has grown leaps & bounds in the last ten to fifteen years, adding new businesses, acquiring companies abroad, recruiting employees with a diverse background—what was needed was a common 'Mahindra' way of working; a framework that would help build a unique 'Mahindra' culture. The idea of Rise has helped us achieve this objective and is now the pivot around which the Group actions revolve."
>
> —S.P. Shukla, President - Group Strategy & Chief Brand Officer, Mahindra & Mahindra Ltd.

Till about a couple of years back employees in various Mahindra Group companies across different business verticals were not able to visualise a common theme that was the sutradhar (common thread) for the group. Recognising this need and based on a study done by Scott Goodsman, from Strawberry Frog, Mahindra launched a transformational change agenda called 'Rise' on 17th January 2011.

Rise is an external re-positioning of the Mahindra Brand and an internal cultural transformation to drive business out performance. It is a concise definition of what Mahindra offers customers and other stakeholders—products, services and solutions that are developed by challenging industry norms, thinking alternatively and combining with customer service standards that meet or exceed expectations that would drive positive change and thus help them to Rise. For Mahindra, Rise means becoming world class in everything they do, setting new benchmarks of excellence, conquering tough global markets and becoming the global number one.

Given the scale of the change envisioned and the transformational potential at hand, there was a strong push towards starting on a firm footing, in a manner that galvanised all stakeholders in the power of Rise. Strawberry Frog, a leading boutique international advertising firm was engaged to conduct a study for the Mahindra Group across the globe with customers, employees and other stakeholders. They discovered group wide common cultural elements and bucketed them into Declining (aspects of the culture that are on the wane), Enduring (aspects of the culture that will always endure) and Emerging (aspects of the culture that are on the rise) sets. Thereafter, the enduring and emerging aspects, Mahindra's unconscious cultural strengths, were clubbed in to form the three Rise pillars of Accepting No Limits, Alternative Thinking and Driving Positive Change.

'Accepting No Limits' is a pillar which represents thinking big and looking beyond conventional boundaries. It encourages employees to be adaptable, agile and to take well-reasoned risks to deliver breakthrough products, services and solutions.

The second Rise Pillar, 'Alternative Thinking', represents new approaches in everyday work-life, seeking out fresh, diverse perspectives and rewarding alternative thinking.

The third Rise pillar, 'Driving Positive Change', focuses on understanding customer needs and offering quality products and services that would not only delight them but also transform their lives.

To take Rise from text to headline, a series of small and large scale workshops were conducted from top management to employees down the line.

To ensure robustness in execution, models like Edgar Schein's model of Organisational Culture, Kotter's Eight Step Change Management Model and the Influence Model were used as strategic frameworks for the change management intervention.

The first kick-off meeting was held on 4 February 2010 with members of the Mahindra HR fraternity across businesses along with senior business leaders, to brainstorm on the first steps for undertaking Rise as a cultural transformation exercise. It was decided that a massive change management program in the form of a holistic, well-rounded OD intervention would be put in place. The first workshop developed towards effectively managing and realising the change, titled "Leading the Brand", was held in early March 2010 to decide on the course of action for developing the spirit of Rise within the Organisation. The workshop served to reveal the enabling and disabling behaviours for each Rise pillar. A key insight that emerged was that the success of the intervention hinged crucially on leaders walking the talk.

To get leadership buy in and to inspire them to propagate the Rise philosophy, a large scale interactive workshop was held at Mumbai with the help of Strawberry Frog on 9th April 2010. The top 300 leaders of the Mahindra Group along with Mr Anand Mahindra (Chairman and Managing Director—Mahindra Group) deliberated and discussed on the theme,

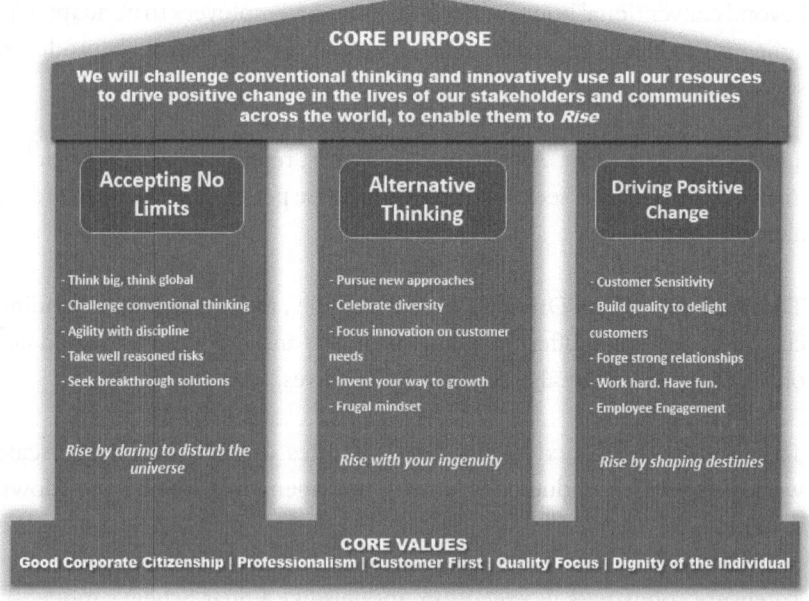

House of Mahindra

with outcomes sorted into affinity buckets which broadly centred around HR and Brand Levers.

Immediately after the workshop, the Office of Strategy Management and key HR leaders deliberated along with senior business leaders to articulate a new core purpose in line with the three pillars of Rise that would reflect the futuristic outlook of the group. The core purpose

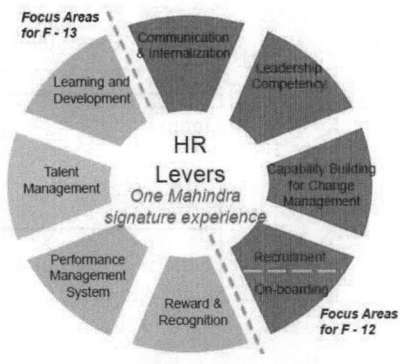

Wheel of Change

was integrated with the three cultural pillars and core values to create a powerful symbol and language called the 'House of Mahindra'. Mahindra Group truly believes that the House of Mahindra will inspire and motivate every employee to achieve its global aspirations.

The outcomes of the three workshops were deliberated by the senior members of the HR fraternity of Mahindra Group to create a three year road-map on re-engineering of HR Processes in line with the Rise philosophy called the Wheel of Change.

Each element of this Wheel of Change was then addressed through a dedicated Project Team as part of the change operationalisation process.

OPERATIONALISING THE CHANGE: BRINGING RISE TO LIFE

The Rise exercise marked a notable shift in Mahindra's core purpose from being a respected Indian conglomerate to a globally recognised brand, which would continually challenge conventional thinking and innovatively use resources to drive positive change, enabling stakeholders and communities to Rise.

To effect the cultural transformation required to realise this change, robust cross functional teams comprising leaders from across the Mahindra group were formed to support the review, design and implementation of the nine key HR processes identified in the Wheel of Change. A dynamic structure was created to execute the change, as part of a detailed three year roadmap. At the top, Rise had the support of the Executive Sponsor,

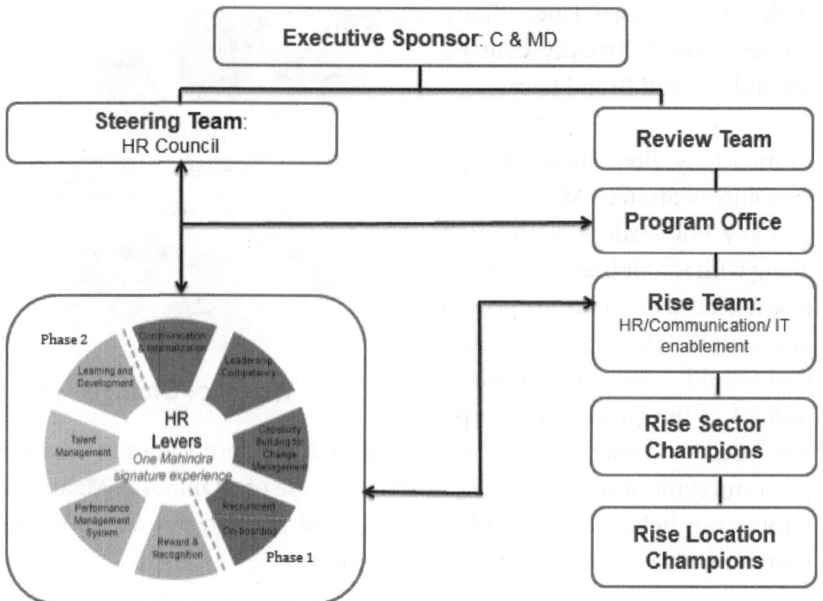

Mr Anand Mahindra, Chairman & MD. Under him, two committees i.e. Steering Team (HR Council) and the Review Team were created to drive the various Rise Initiatives in the human resource domain.

To ensure alignment and to drive execution, the Program Office was setup as a separate entity, reporting to the HR Council and the Review Team. The Rise Team(a change management team), was integrated into Group HR to support the Program Office to review various Rise HR Projects. The Rise Team which comprised of the Rise HR Projects teams and the digital communication and employer branding teams in line with Rise tenets, had a consulting role to offer to all the other project teams. Apart from these, Sector Champions and Location Champions were chosen to assist in Rise related initiatives for each sector. The projects are reviewed every month by the Program Office and every quarter by the HR Council.

Rise was formally launched by Mr Anand Mahindra in mid—January 2011 across the group and a digital platform was created to support the change initiative so that the stories of the three pillars were captured and employee aspirations were disseminated through it.

Different businesses within the Mahindra Group then cascaded the change initiatives down the line, engaging with employees at a more proximal level, addressing specific queries and concerns while always linking the agenda back to the larger Mahindra picture. These efforts included award ceremonies, orientation sessions, participative events such as quizzes, competitions, blogs, etc.

DESIGNING A COMMUNICATION STRATEGY AND ENSURING SOUND FEEDBACK

In Mahindra's endeavour to communicate and document feedback for the effectiveness of the Rise Campaign, a number of major communication initiatives were implemented across the organisation. This included a Large Scale Interactive Process (LSIP) aimed at creating and propagating a shared understanding of the Rise philosophy across businesses and locations.

Another very effective bottom-up communication platform involved online chats conducted between senior Mahindra leaders and employees across levels, locations and geographies at a designated time and date. This helped in cutting through hierarchical boundaries, securing employee buy-in, and ensured two-way communication enabling a culture that promotes transparency and openness.

Given the deep-rooted drivers to be impacted for success in bringing about the desired change, an Annual Engagement Survey was also conducted incorporating specific questions gauging the efficacy of the change efforts.

MANAGING INITIAL RESISTANCE

The biggest challenge faced by Mahindra Group post initiation of Rise was to create a common understanding of the Rise Imperatives in a federated structure comprising eighteen diverse businesses, each of which were at different stages of maturity. In view of these challenges, the team designed and deployed interventions aligned with Kotter's eight-step process for Leading Change, as summarised below:

Each of these steps was implemented through a diverse array of initiatives, including large scale interactive processes, focus group discussions,

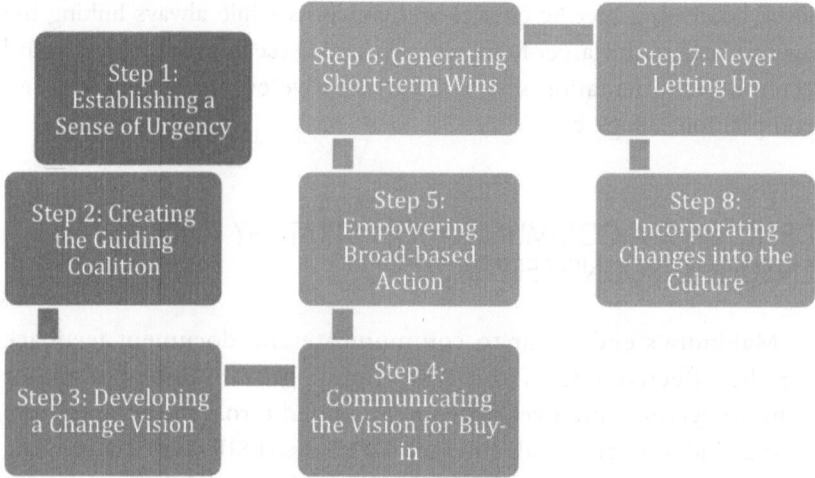

training—orientation sessions, targeted influencer orientations, mass engagement activities (such as competitions, anthems, etc.), among several others.

The in-depth feedback mechanisms discussed earlier also served to nip several possible areas of resistance early enough in the game, allowing the organisation to minimise the drag of passive / inertial resistance, and stride forward on its transformational journey.

INSTITUTIONALISING THE CHANGE TO ENSURE IT STUCK

Using Rewards and Recognition as a potent mean for reinforcing desired attitudes and behaviours had formed an integral part of the Rise change strategy. Thus an end-to-end awards process was put in place, wherein any employee / team within Mahindra could submit their Rise stories. A jury comprising business leaders would then evaluate the stories and winners were selected for each Rise pillar at a business, sector and group level.

An interactive digital platform was also launched in January 2012 to develop the brand positioning of Rise and unify the group under the Rise philosophy. Some of the key features of the portal included games, media gallery, brand centre, among others—all designed to better engage the employees with the overarching message and vision of Rise.

Having kick-started the Rise journey just a year back, the group articulated its global aspiration as under:

"We aim to make 'Mahindra' one of the 50 most admired Global Brands by 2021."

THE IMPACT OF RISE

The completion of the projects slated for the first year of the Wheel of Change led to more robust and better aligned systems being instated in the areas of communication & internalization, leadership competency development, capability building for change management and recruitment/on-boarding. The new Mahindra Group Leadership competencies have been incorporated in the other HR Levers to provide the One Mahindra signature experience as depicted below:

The second year projects have led to a broad-based evolution of key processes in the areas of Learning & Development, Talent Management, Performance Management and Rewards & Recognition.

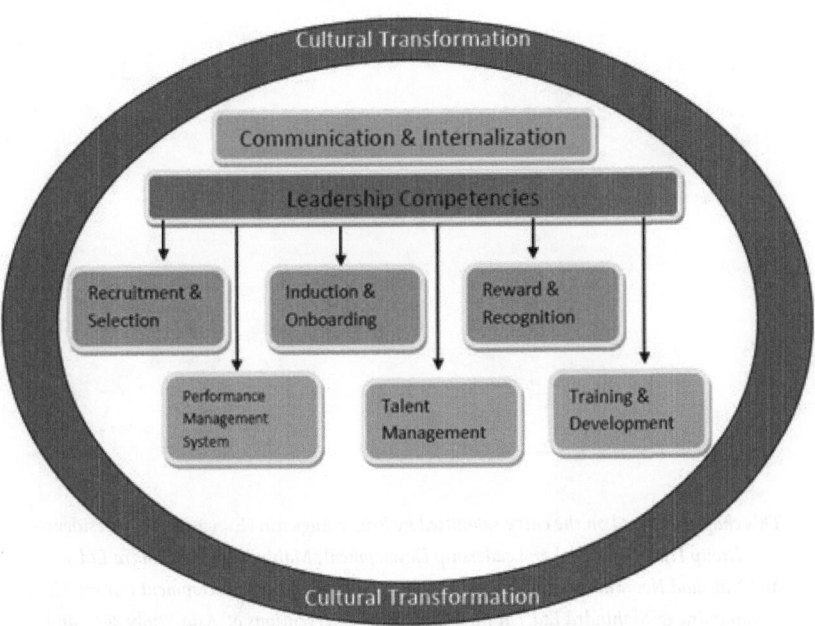

All in all, the Rise initiative has impacted almost 1,55,000 employees of Mahindra Group in 100 countries, spread across 18 eighteen industries. More than 20,000 employees were covered through online and offline channels on Mahindra Leadership Competencies. The Rise Portal in particular was extremely well received with almost 500,000 page visits. The Revenue for Mahindra Group grew by thirty per cent from 12.5 billion US dollars (in FY 2011) to 16.2 billion US dollars (FY 2013)—which were remarkable achievements given a recessionary macroeconomic environment globally.

Several National and International accolades were also bestowed upon the Mahindra Group post implementation of Rise. These include, the "'Most Innovative Company Award' from Business Standard, the 'Business Leader Lifetime Achievement' and 'Leader in Automotive (4 four wheeler) Award' from NDTV Profit and the prestigious 'Boldness in Business Award—Emerging Markets' from Arcelor Mittal. Rise has indeed been very effective in establishing Mahindra as a respected and innovative global brand, committed to positively impacting the lives of stakeholders and the external environment.

This chapter is based on the entry submitted by Prince Augustin (Executive Vice President—Group Human Capital & Leadership Development, Mahindra & Mahindra Ltd.) and Naushad Noorani (Senior General Manager—Organisation Development (Group HR), Mahindra & Mahindra Ltd.) at the Best Change Interventions of Asia Study 2012 and cannot be reproduced without the expressed permission of Mahindra & Mahindra Ltd.

What Mahindra did differently to successfully manage and drive change

The Rise Campaign was an external repositioning of the Mahindra Brand which was conceptualised with the objective of making Mahindra a word-class organisation and a market leader in each of the sectors it operated in.

- The Group engaged an external advertising firm to identify group wide common cultural elements into three broad categories (Declining, Enduring and Emerging). The enduring and emerging aspects when then clubbed together to form Mahindra's three Rise pillars.

- Key focus areas were identified to address potential derailers of the change agenda with detailed descriptors and timelines.

- The group created a three year roadmap on re-engineering HR Processes in line with the Rise philosophy. A total of nine project teams were set up to standardise and reflect Rise behaviours in core HR processes and ensure focussed attention and sustenance of implemented initiatives,

- The group accordingly identified and articulated a pan Mahindra Group Leadership Competency Framework which was integrated with all HR levers and processes. The Rise behaviours were also extended to ensure recruitment of the right talent, facilitate a quality induction process , institutionalise a coherent Rewards and Recognition framework and a robust Performance Management System

- The group benchmarked more than thirty organisations on how they managed their talent. This included talent identification, talent segmentation and talent development stages. Subsequently a complete 'As Is' audit was conducted and key deliverables were assigned to bridge the gaps identified.

- To manage the change efforts the Mahindra Group drew heavily from Kotter's eight step Change Model, organised large scale focus group discussions across locations and also ensured that change efforts were communicated down the line through Large Scale Interactive Processes.

- The change management journey at Mahindra Group has progressed very rapidly with key stakeholders ensuring that change efforts undertaken were sustained and institutionalised. Rise has indeed been very effective in establishing Mahindra as a respected and innovative global brand, committed to positively impacting the lives of stakeholders and the external environment.

Lessons for Change Managers

The Mahindra story presents key lessons for change managers conceptualising and driving interventions in organisations:

- Identifying organisational capabilities and aligning them with internal policies/ processes is essential for percolating the larger organisational values by identifying and influencing all touch-points.

- Ensuring buy-in of key stakeholders to drive adoption and long term sustenance of change efforts is critical for change managers. Assigning a senior leader/ key stakeholder as the sponsor of the intervention is particularly useful to facilitate this.

- Sharing success stories through the many available communication channels aligns the workforce with larger organisational goals. This re-iterates key success factors and desirable behaviours which contribute to enhance Employeeship across the organisation.

EXTENDING THE HORIZON FOR CHANGE THROUGH BUSINESS

TRANSFOR-MATION

The PNB Housing Finance Ltd Story

"Change will not come if we wait for some other person or some other time. We are the ones we've been waiting for. We are the change that we seek"

—Barack Obama

COMPANY PROFILE

PNB Housing Finance Limited (PNB HFL) is a registered housing finance company with National Housing Bank (NHB). It commenced its operations on 11 November, 1988 as a fully owned subsidiary of Punjab National Bank (PNB). On 9 December, 2009, it entered into a strategic financial partnership with Destimoney Enterprises Private Limited (DEPL), today PNB's ownership is at fifty-one per cent and that of strategic partner at forty-nine per cent.

PNB HFL currently employs 405 employees and had annual revenue figures of INR 463 crores (USD 74.9 million USD) (for FY 2011–12) and INR 661 crores (106.6 million USD) (for FY 2012–13).

CREATING URGENCY AROUND A VISION FOR CHANGE

PNB Housing Finance Limited (PNB HFL) had been in existence since 1988 as a fully owned subsidiary of Punjab National Bank (PNB)—India's third largest bank in terms of assets. A mono-line company whose primary product included providing home loan and other mortgage products, the organisation had experienced stagnant business growth with a market share of less than 0.4per cent since its inception. This was in sharp contrast to peers from the industry who had grown rapidly in wake of liberalization measures of 1991 that had positively impacted the financial services sector in India.

As a fully owned subsidiary of a large nationalised commercial bank the workforce of PNB HFL constituted of employees on deputation from Punjab National Bank (who mostly held the senior positions) and a pool of management cadre recruited through an all India recruitment examination. The need of having key functional roles including demarcating Sales and Credit, institutionalising a dedicated Sales and Distribution setup at the Branch and Head Office(HO) levels, creating specialised roles for performance excellence and having a clearly articulated role and reporting matrix was widely felt by the management.

The organisation had experienced instances of diffused focus on key functional areas due to lack of specialised functions and misaligned reporting relationships (which led to situations like IT-Hardware reporting to HR, IT-Software reporting to Finance and Recovery, Legal reporting to Marketing). Moreover there was an absence of a structured and transparent Performance Management System resulting in a deficit orientation on performance / business excellence among employees. This led to excessive decentralization at the same time making the head office's span of control substantially large and negating the positive impact of empowering individual SBUs.

Inspite of the company being in existence for twenty-two years they had achieved marginal success. Office matters were looking bleak and desperate for the employees of the organisation and for the company itself. The company had a small loan book of less than INR 2,000 crore (322.6 million USD) and annual incremental business of less than INR 700 crore (112.9 million USD). Employees and stake holders knew that the existing business model had failed miserably—companies with the same vintage had a ten times bigger portfolio, better human capital policies and profitability. There were also strong talks in PNB corridors about the eminent merger with the parent bank; which meant a lot of uncertainties and testing times for the 140 odd employees.

In 2009–10, the Board of PNB HFL decided to explore the possibility of a "Public Private Partnership" (PPP) by liquidating the stake to a Private Equity (PE) with the objective of re-engineering the business and transforming the organisational culture. As part of the stakeholder agreement the deputies from Punjab National Bank were repatriated and the management undertook a concerted effort to develop a structured talent pipeline by hiring fresh talent across levels, from the industry. The project was named 'Kshitij' (derived from the Hindi word meaning horizon—where the earth and the sky meet").

The objective of project 'Kshitij' was to embark upon a business transformation exercise to incorporate best-in-class internal processes, policies, to bring about functional expertise by hiring top talent from the industry and to take targeted steps to upgrade the skill sets of the existing talent pool. The project aimed at improving the market position of PNB Housing Finance Ltd by positioning the brand as an aggressive profit generating corporate enterprise providing stability and credibility usually associated with a Public Sector Undertaking (PSU).

INITIAL RESISTANCE

While Punjab National Bank was an established brand, there was limited awareness of PNBHFL as an employer, at a time when the organisation was making concerted efforts to hire top talent from the market to build in-house functional capabilities. There were general apprehensions among employees against the new management which were further accentuated by a strong grapevine leading to wide-spread anxiety and disorientation.

The primary challenge faced during the business transformation exercise was hiring top talent and managing the business and cultural change process for new hires and existing employees at the same time establishing and re-emphasising the credibility of the new management. This would then be complemented by integrating and amalgamating old employees with new hires to bring about a performance—excellence driven culture, rewarding individual and collective performance.

PNB Housing Finance Ltd's mission was to establish itself as a most preferred housing finance company, making the experience of owning a house stress-free and simple. Aspirationally the enterprise aim to achieve a position amongst the market leaders on a pan India basis by acquiring a loan book of INR 35,000 crores (USD 5.64 billion) by FY 2017–18 and to be viewed as an employer of choice.

TAKING DIRECTED STEPS TOWARDS OPERATIONALISING THE CHANGE

Business transformation committees comprising of representatives across grades and functions were formed at PNB HFL to understand employee aspirations and existing organisational challenges. The recommendations of the committees were then taken to the Board of Directors to explain the need and urgency for business and organisational transformation. Globally renowned management consultant KPMG was empanelled as a consulting partner to facilitate the transformation process and support identification of gaps in processes, policies, practices and the organisation structure by providing relevant recommendations. This led to the creation of a detailed road-map for business transformation with timelines being allocated to specific milestones complemented by periodic review of key deliverables.

DESIGNING A COMMUNICATION STRATEGY AND ENSURING SOUND FEEDBACK MECHANISMS

The Management realised that communicating the need for undergoing a business transformation exercise to all the employees early in the game was essential for securing employee buy-in and bring about sustainable organisational and cultural change. The existing employee base was subdivided into three categories and were identified as 'Change enablers' comprising of about twenty per cent of the employees who were aligned with the change process and about fifty to sixty per cent employees were 'Fence sitters' who were adopting a wait and watch policy keenly observing how the future will unfold. Balance were 'Lost cases', who were completely against the change and the management. To manage initial resistance, key influencers were identified across locations as Change Champions.

Each Change Champion was provided a detailed overview of the vision for change and the need for a business transformation exercise. Steps were taken to ensure regular engagement of change champions with the senior management thereby making them a connecting link between the management and the employees. The disoriented/ cynical employees (defined as lost cases) were geographically segregated and assigned to members of the leadership team, who were made responsible for engaging them and ensuring retention.

A number of town halls were conducted across locations by the leadership team to communicate the roll out of new policies and to monitor milestones associated with the business transformation exercise. With an aim to re-establish trust and credibility, an open door policy was introduced to facilitate interactions with the Management including the Managing Director, Mr Sanjaya Gupta. Other innovative communication channels like 'Sampark', MD's Address were also announced to ensure top-down communication throughout the organisation. During the MD's address, questions/concerns (both live and anonymous) were compiled and addressed by Mr Sanjaya Gupta (Managing Director—PNB Housing Finance Ltd). An innovative email based communication channel (MD's post) offered employees the opportunity to put forward their concerns/ queries directly to the Managing Director. In addition, employee representatives were often selected and invited to attend board meetings which provided them a detailed overview of the financial performance of PNB HFL and future course of action adopted by the company.

MANAGING INITIAL RESISTANCE AND INSTITUTIONALISING THE CHANGE TO ENSURE IT WAS SUSTAINED

In order to imbibe the PNB HFL DNA among employees 'Mission, Vision and Values' workshops was conducted. The workshops aimed at ensuring participation of management teams, the Board of Directors and employee representatives across grades. The participants were induced to arrive at values which could be reflected in day to day employee behaviours—this would in turn lead to the building of a "Value Based Company" rather than a 'Rule Based Company' at PNB HFL.

The company objectives, strategy and expectations were elucidated through the available communication channels and by the Change Champions. At pre-designated milestones, town-halls were periodically organised to invite opinions, views and feedback from the employees by addressing individual and collective concerns. A new market aligned HR policy was also incorporated with best practices from the industry.

To bring about a transparent and performance driven culture, a formal Performance Management System (PMS) was institutionalised and key deliverables were defined for individuals and functions leading to meaningful empowerment for all. This was accompanied by the launch of Reward and Recognition programs across the organisation.

The Best talent in the mortgage industry were hired in leadership positions, with strong coaching and mentoring skill sets being a critical competency during the Talent Acquisition process. Development centres were also conducted to identify core competencies and skill sets to ensure optimal job/role fitment. Extensive skill up-gradation programs, cross functional training programs were conducted to bridge prevailing technical/functional gaps leading to enhanced business results.

Team bonding initiatives were periodically conducted to integrate existing employees and new hires. In addition workshops on 'Stress Management' and talks by eminent change management experts and spiritual leaders were conducted to address the emotional turbulence.

Both successes and failures were collectively recognised ensuring accountability at all levels. PNBHFL's leadership team displayed exemplary commitment to maintaining transparency, adherence to timelines and enabling the participation of employees across levels in the decision making process. This positively impacted the credibility of the new management and fostered a climate of trust, pride and commitment to achieving business results.

IMPACT ON THE BUSINESS

The business transformation exercise of PNBHFL positively impacted the financial results of the company (observed from FY 2010–11 to FY 2011–12) which led to a twenty-seven per cent increase in total income, a twenty-five per cent increase in portfolio, a nineteen per cent increase in new loan disbursement and a 0.67 per cent reduction of net NPA (Non-performing Assets). The financial results of the company (i.e. from FY 2011–12 to FY 2012–13) indicate a forty-three per cent increase in total income, a sixty-seven per cent increase in portfolio, a staggering 142 per cent increase in new loan disbursement and net Non-Performing Assets (NPA) reduced to 0.35% (best in industry benchmark).

"Today, we cherish the solidity of our parent organization and the tenacity to improvise a contemporary sales model to reach out to our customers and to serve them with élan and the robustness of a caring organisation. We believe this is only the beginning of a strong foundation, upon which a sustainable and profitable financial super-house would be built with strong values of People First, Costumer Centric and Ethical Standards."

—Shaji Varghese, Business Head—PNB Housing Finance Ltd.

PNB Housing Finance Ltd was also awarded the 'Outstanding Contribution to Real Estate Sector through Growth in Home Loans—North India' at the third Annual Real Estate Awards and the 'Outstanding Contribution to Real Estate sector through Growth in Home Loans—West India' at the fourth Annual Real Estate Awards organised by Franchise India.

PNB Housing Finance Limited received a CRISIL AA/ positive Bank Loan Long Term Rating and a CRISIL AA/Stable and Care AA+ rating on Bonds. In addition, the commercial paper program and fixed deposit program received CRISIL A1+ and FAA+/Stable ratings respectively.

The Human Capital ratios for FY 2013–14 too have been very impressive with the ROI on Human Capital recorded at INR 26.56 (ROI is the revenue earned excluding operating expenses for every rupee invested in human capital) and Human Capital Value Added and Revenue per Employee at INR 2.15 crores (346,000 USD) and INR 2.29 crores (369,000 USD).

The business transformation exercise—Project 'Kshitij' led to PNB Housing Finance Ltd establishing itself amongst the leading players in the Housing Finance Sector with 'Best in Industry' financial results. This was undoubtedly an outcome of outstanding change management and communication initiatives by the Management which secured employee buy-in across the organisation and helped align individual performances to achieve overall business results.

This chapter is based on the entry submitted by Anshul Bhargava (Chief People Officer—PNB Housing Finance Ltd.) and Satish Kumar Singh (Senior Manager—Human Resources, PNB Housing Finance Ltd.) at the Best Change Interventions of Asia Study 2012

What PNB HFL did differently to successfully manage and drive change

PNB Housing Finance Ltd undertook a business transformation exercise (christened Project *Kshitij*) to enhance market share and build capabilities among employees. The Financial institution—once a fully owned subsidiary of an established Public Sector Bank, was operating via the Public Private Partnership model since 2009–10 and needed to reposition itself as a leading player in the financial services sector.

- The existing employee base was categorised basis estimated engagement levels (measured in terms of perceived alignment) post implementation of Project Kshitij. To manage initial resistance key influencers were identified and earmarked as Change Champions.

- Disoriented and cynical employees were geographically segregated and assigned to members of the leadership team who were made responsible for their engagement and involvement.

- Regular communication mechanisms were undertaken in the form of periodic town-halls, the MD's address and an innovative email based communication channel christened MD's post.

- The company's objectives and strategy was elucidated across the organisation by change champions—a new HR policy was institutionalised to incorporate best practices from the industry.

- A formal Performance Management System was set up to align individual goals with business objectives. This was followed by the launch of a new Rewards and Recognition program across the organisation.

- The best talent from the mortgage industry were hired in leadership positions. Extensive skill up gradation programs were conducted to bridge observed technical/ functional/ development gaps of employees.

- Project *Kshitij* positively impacted the financial results of PNB Housing Finance Ltd and won the organisation a number of national and international accolades. It also established the organisation as a leading player in the mortgage industry having recorded exceptional financial performance with regards net NPA and new loan disbursements.

Lessons for Change Managers

The PNB Housing Finance Ltd story presents the following lessons for change managers conceptualising and driving change interventions in organisations:

- A detailed project plan with timelines and key milestones must be created and periodically tracked post inception of the business transformation agenda.

- Hiring best in class talent and amalgamating new employees with existing employees to bring about a performance driven culture which celebrates collective successes is critical to create a performance oriented meritocracy.

- Robust communication mechanisms are key to negate the adverse impact of strong grapevines arising due to uncertainties and apprehensions associated with the transformation exercise. Leaders must play a key role in clearly articulating the organisation's vision and long term strategy by using various channels for targeted communication.

- Change Champions need to be assigned across functions and business units to build a climate of trust, pride and commitment. Disoriented employees must be identified early in the game and assigned mentors for addressing challenges associated with engagement and contribution.

- Both successes and failures must be acknowledged collectively ensuring accountability at all levels. Adherence to timelines for achievement of milestones and ensuring inclusion and participation of employees at all levels is key for enabling adoption for change.

PROSPERITY THROUGH VALUES FOR SUSTAIN-ABLE GROWTH

The SAIL Story

"First comes thought; then organization of that thought, into ideas and plans; then transformation of those plans into reality. The beginning, as you will observe is in your imagination"

—Napoleon Hill

COMPANY PROFILE

सेल SAIL

Steel Authority of India Limited (SAIL) is among the leading steel producers in India. It is a fully integrated iron and steel maker, producing both basic and special steels for domestic construction, engineering, power, railway, automotive, and defence industries and for sale in export markets. It is also among the seven *Maharatnas* (Prominent Jewel) of the country's central public sector enterprises. SAIL has the distinction of being India's second largest producer of iron ore and of having the country's second largest mines network. The company's vision is *'To be a respected world class corporation and the leader in Indian steel business in quality, productivity, profitability and customer satisfaction'*.

SAIL has been through its long journey so far with many a crest and trough on the way. Each of its plants and units have shown resilience and perseverance, and gained the stature and command of being the industry leader as SAIL collective. This is the transformation story of Rourkela Steel Plant (RSP). RSP was the first integrated steel plant in the public sector in India, set up with German collaboration. RSP has the capacity to produce two million tonnes of hot metal, 1.9 million tonnes of crude steel and 1.67 million tonnes of saleable steel. It is SAIL's only plant that produces silicon steels for the power sector, high quality pipes for the oil & gas sector and tin plates for the packaging industry. Its wide and sophisticated product range includes various flat, tubular and coated products.

SAIL ROURKELA STEEL PLANT IN A TOUGH BUSINESS ENVIRONMENT

Market and industry turbulence in the late nineties was sending aftershocks in the Indian manufacturing setup, posing a threat for capital intensive organisations looking for breakeven. The Indian manufacturing industry in general and the steel industry in particular were suffering the consequences of a severe recession which had hit India in 1998 and continued till 2002. The steel industry was further hit with a double pincer of low demand and overcapacity, as all steel majors had invested heavily in capacity expansion just prior to the bust. Rourkela Steel Plant was burdened with large financial overheads of servicing a debt of Rs 4000 crores (645 million USD) for the modernization project; at a time when both the sales volume and prices were low. Low capacity utilization in a capital intensive industry meant that RSP had been steadily making losses since the early nineties, which had been further aggravated after modernization added to the financial overheads.

There had been an influx of over 5,000 contract labourers on the rolls of the company in the early nineties as a result of a court ruling that changed the IR dynamics of the plant. The authority of the plant managers, as a result had been seriously challenged, with the dominant union now holding a strong influence on events. The workforce morale was at an all time low and there was constant apprehension about the future of RSP and also the township which was dependent solely on the plant for its economy. While the flagship plants of Bhilai and Bokaro had started turning around, the financial results of Rourkela were a drag on the overall profitability of SAIL. The overwhelming odds against achieving profitability had broken the spirit and confidence of most employees. There was a feeling of helplessness about the ability to turn things around; employees blamed external factors for the state of affairs.

The SAIL management planned to bring things back on track by channeling the collective energy to contribute and take up ownership within the organisation. The management sought a two-pronged approach—of bridging communication gaps in the organisation and building a leadership pipeline capable of dealing with challenging business and economic scenarios.

THE MASS CONTACT EXERCISE: INITIATING GROUND-LEVEL CHANGE

A Mass Contact Exercise was envisaged, aimed at rebuilding a culture of ownership, commitment and accountability, using direct communication with the entire workforce as a lever for driving change. This initiative continues as an ongoing and institutionalised process at RSP to this date, having been initiated on 19 April 2002. It was designed with the objective of creating a mass movement aimed at aligning the workforce with organisational goals, breaking barriers between minds and turning the 'locus of control' inwards, making employees feel responsible for their own future and the future of the plant. This initiative has also helped develop a culture of transparency and information sharing, building trust among teams and departments.

The exercise was rolled out to all employees of the RSP, in batches of around 500 employees at a time. The meetings, held every Wednesday, were presided by the top management of RSP to encourage sharing of feedback, concerns and expectations by employees. The quorum called for the CEO and other members of the top management of RSP to be present without exception, with a dedicated group directly reporting to the CEO, responsible for documenting all the issues raised and taking follow up action. These meetings also included presentations by the management on the state of the company, and RSP in particular, with facts, figures and contextual explanations. Each such meeting would end with the employees undertaking a pledge to build a sustainable work environment and commit to the success of the company. This pledge was later cemented as RSP's credo called 'Samskar'(Culture).

This initiative was unprecedented in its attempt at connecting with employees on the issues most deeply impacting business. The active participation of the leadership meant there was a sense of urgency generated, while robust follow-through on action plans lent the entire exercise some degree of credence. As we will see, the Mass Contact Exercise underwent several evolutionary shifts as acceptance and participation increased, with the perseverance and commitment of the management serving as the essential backbone for change to succeed.

OVERCOMING INITIAL RESISTANCE TO OPEN COMMUNICATION

Steeped in a rigid, hierarchical culture, and influenced by the workforce unions on most matters relating to work life, the organisation wasn't exactly well placed for such an initiative. However, given the situation RSP found itself in, and the dire need for performance turnaround, which in turn could only follow culture change, the management was more than committed to the task at hand.

The forum had a tentative start with the dominant union vehemently opposing it. Perceived as an intrusion on their turf, the union made all efforts to stop employees from participating. Targeted efforts were made towards reassuring and persuading employees to attend the meetings, which eventually succeeded as the forum grew to fulfill its potential as an opportunity to connect with the last man standing. With management assurance that no bipartite issues would be addressed through the forum, the unions also joined into this vital, potentially life-saving initiative for RSP.

ENABLING THE INITIATIVE TO EVOLVE FOR MEANINGFUL CHANGE

The forum evolved at multiple levels over the years, adapting to changes in the organisational context and market dynamics. In the early days, the Mass Contact events effectively served as forums where employees could vent their grievances, concerns and emotions freely in an open atmosphere. The first few months were therefore quite cathartic for most employees. At this stage, the management stance was clear—acknowledge employees' feelings without getting defensive; encourage free expression of thoughts and feelings while being open about existing challenges and pressing responsibilities, ensuring the context is never lost. Sincere efforts were made to address every issue raised, without judgment on relevance to or appropriateness for the forum. The guiding principle was 'If it is legal, and it can be done, we should do it'. This phase saw the discussions shifting from raw venting of emotions and biases to opening up on personal matters impacting satisfaction and work performance.

As time passed, with issues both personal and professional getting at least a fair hearing, if not meaningful resolution, there was greater trust that germinated and grew in the forum. This was built upon to bring workplace issues out into the open, in an open non-threatening manner. Regular flow of information on key issues such as productivity, costs, profitability, production, breakdowns, etc. began to register with the employees, slowly shifting the conversations towards the plant, serving to identify systemic and process weaknesses affecting the organisation adversely. Even though the tone still expressed an external locus of control among employees, often playing the blame game, this phase saw much corrective action being taken towards deep-rooted causes of employee complaints. This led to a significant improvement in the company's service quality and strengthened its perception as a caring employer.

With more frequent and in-depth discussions around key challenges facing the plant, and stringent follow-up on action plans formed thereof, employees gradually started seeing their own roles in the successes and failures of different initiatives, thus eliciting a sense of accountability and ownership. Over time therefore, the tone of the conversations shifted to individual and collective responsibility, with a more solutions orientation. This was an inflection point for the Mass Contact Exercise.

With growing trust, openness and accountability, the forum now focused on proactively identifying areas and processes with a scope for optimization. Any issues hampering plant operations and efficiency were now everybody's business. Over time, the conversations evolved further to the sharing of best practices and celebration of achievements from across the plant. This public recognition induced a sense of belonging and pride towards the organisation and RSP, in sharp contrast to the atmosphere not so long ago.

SUSTAINING THE CHANGE WITH CULTURAL EVOLUTION

To infuse a value system in tune with the desired culture of ownership and contribution, a unique value aligning exercise was carried out through a movement called *'SAMSKAR'*(Cultural Heritage*)*, which later on came to be recognised as the vision of RSP. The process started with a pledge that was taken in every Mass Contact Exercise—*"The future of our steel Plant lies in our hands. It is our individual and collective responsibility to rebuild our Plant into a profitable, harmonious and vibrant organisation. We will do whatever things are necessary, which are good for our Plant. We shall never do anything that hurts our Plant."*

This pledge was reinforced across the organisation through a communication campaign across all official forums as a demonstration of the employee commitment to turn around plant performance. By accepting accountability for individual actions, RSP further refined this message into a credo in the form of a prayer *'SAMSKAR'*—*"We have to create and sustain a peaceful work environment where every employee can contribute to the plant in the assigned area of work with full freedom and dignity and without fear"*. The statement was crafted after much deliberation to capture the essence of the desired culture at Rourkela. Through this tone, the message was targeted at the cultural moorings of the workforce by invoking their pride in their culture, heritage and social values. The survival of Rourkela Steel Plant had to be connected to the survival of a deeply held *way of life*. Employees had to see the plant not just as a factory but the foundation of a social system.

SAMSKAR became the cultural foundation of Rourkela Steel Plant as the company made cultural and operational improvements, and was further reinforced with the new credo statements reflecting the evolving aspirations of the Rourkela Steel Plant collective. After carving out a new and distinctive identity, RSP commenced on a new journey towards exploring fresh vistas of positivity and crafted *SAMRIDHI* (Prosperity), which was in the form of the following statements of affirmation.

SAMRIDHI (Prosperity)

- Our strength: Sustenance of their *Samskar (Cultural Heritage)* by employees with their unlimited potential.

- Our pride: A culture that fosters dignity and encourages transparency, trust and togetherness

- Our SAIL RSP's objectives: Achieving total safety, perfect quality, optimum costs and maximum productivity in a harmonious environment.
  Our Sankalp (Resolve) is to spread Samridhi

This statement was further refined in 2012 with a new aspiration *SAMVARDHAN* (Sustainable Growth). The word carries a much nuanced meaning which may be difficult to capture in English, but literally translates to 'cultivation, development, promotion, augmentation, enrichment'. It carries the new aspirations of Rourkela Steel Plant, which is now a confident unit searching for new avenues for excellence.

SAMVARDHAN (Sustainable Growth)

- Samskriti *(which means Culture):* Reinforcing a culture of safety, environment, quality and cost consciousness by converting awareness into action

---

- Samprasaran *(which means Expansion):* Reaping the benefits of expansion by galvanising every mind
- Spandan *(which means Vibrancy):* Making every workplace a haven of vibrancy and fulfillment
- Samanway *(which means Synergy):* Achieving total synergy by creating a symbiotic relation with each valued partner

  Let us spread Samriddhi (Prosperity) through our Samskar (Culture) and accomplish Samvardhan (Sustainable Growth)

The journey from *SAMSKAR* to *SAMVARDHAN* marks RSP's growth as it increasingly gained confidence. The forum started with throwing open a challenge for improvement in operational parameters and generating cash profits, since net profit seemed unattainable. By 2004–05 however, RSP had achieved Net Profit after eight years of losses, with the <u>highest ever sales turnover</u> thus far. It then evolved into developing systems and processes with a focus on maintenance and reinforcement of basic operative systems, while continuing to address personal grievances and recognising achievers.

This journey also highlights the ***paradoxical nature of change with continuity*** that has been managed at RSP as it continues to evolve till date.

Complementary Initiatives

The Mass Contact Exercise proved to be a fulcrum for a larger exercise of aligning the workforce with the organisational agenda, supported by many other initiatives.

i. **GMCM (General Managers Communication Meeting) and HoDs (Head of Departments) Communication Meeting**

   In due course, complementary communication forums were developed at lower levels with a view to make communication and sharing of purpose all pervasive. A two tiered communication mechanism was institutionalised:

   - **HoDs Communication Meetings**—Meetings with cross sections of employees from the department chaired by the Head of the Department, to sort out issues and address concerns. They had a smaller scope (within the department).

   - **GMCM (General Managers Communication Meeting)**—Forums

chaired by a General Manager who would be in charge of more than one department.

All GMs and departmental heads now worked out their own communication calendars to ensure that they too covered all their employees. Through this process of cascaded communication forums, a greater line of sight was established along with a detailed understanding of ground-level issues. This led to a strong alignment of workforce and an increased sense of ownership and action.

ii. **Workshops on Leadership Practices**

The CEO realised that in the face of challenges caused by macro and micro factors, building a leadership pipeline was a critical imperative. He worked on concretising the role of the leader through the five modules of the leadership practices identified—*SAMSKAR*, Empowerment, Safety, a culture of Family orientation and Preventive maintenance at the workplace; reflecting the priorities of RSP.

iii. **Performance Improvement Workshops**

Performance improvement workshops were organised for employees from different departments to address issues holding back production and productivity. The emotional energy unleashed by the Mass Contact was harnessed through these workshops, resulting in system and work practice (innovation) improvements that cumulatively saved RSP hundreds of crores in cost.

THE IMPACT ON ROURKELA STEEL PLANT

The outcomes of this process have been inspiring and even led to similar exercises being tried in other plants and units of SAIL. Some of the outcomes below capture the quantum of change RSP has seen over the last eleven years:

- Financially from net losses of over 1300 crores (209.7 million USD) in 2001–02, Rourkela has moved to a profit of 1076 crores (173.5 million USD) in 2004–05 and has been retaining this level of profitability ever since.
- Hot metal production has in increased from levels of 1.3 MTPA (Million Tonnes per annum) to levels of 2.2 MTPA in 2011–12 in a Plant with rated capacity of two MTPA
- Crude steel production has increased from levels of 1.3 MTPA in 2001–02 to over 2.2 MTPA in 2011–12

- Saleable Steel production has increased from levels of 1.3 MTPA in 2001–02 to over 2.0 MTPA in 2011–12

As would be evident from these figures, the capacity utilization has been tremendously increased to levels beyond 100 per cent, up from around sixty-seven per cent in 2001–02. The techno-economics of the plant have also improved tremendously in all the major operations and RSP boasts of the best SAIL figures on many such parameters. For its stellar performance, the plant has won many national awards in many areas like environment management, energy management etc.

"The Mass contact exercise symbolises the vibrant spirit of SAIL RSP. It is the ship on which we sail to achieve our collective dreams for our company and our nation. Through this forum the RSP collective has emerged stronger and more united with every challenge that it has faced. The endeavour to build a great company, driven by the collective passion of people ever ready for change, has significantly supported this initiative. The Mass Communication Exercise is a victory of the belief that changes are embraced and not resisted when we appeal to the core values of our people and respect voices from the grassroots."

—Sanjay Dhar, Sr. Faculty Member—Management Training Institute, SAIL

The real transformational change has been in the mindset of RSP collective, and the confidence that it has generated. Since the gloomy days of yore, it has not only grown to be a star performing plant for SAIL, but also became the nurturing ground for future leaders of SAIL, with many leaders in key positions across SAIL having evolved through the tumultuous years since 2002. From being a plant plagued with militant unionism, it has moved on to have one of the most productive workforces across SAIL and an industrial climate marked by complete harmony.

The Mass Contact Exercise is a unique example of using a communication forum as a platform for driving a cultural change. It demonstrates how sharing concerns, generating collective commitment for the future and bringing closeness among people can make transformational change happen. This journey of change and progress is a journey of going far by reducing the distances between minds, as the RSP story continues forward.

This chapter is based on the entry submitted by Manas Ranjan Panda (Executive Director—HRD, Steel Authority of India Ltd.) and Sanjay Dhar (Sr. Faculty Member, Management Training Institute, Steel Authority of India Ltd.) at the Best Change Interventions of Asia Study 2012

What SAIL did differently to successfully manage and drive change

The SAIL Rourkela Steel Plant (RSP) managed to turn itself around from a state of chronic losses to consistent, robust profitability, through a concerted change intervention rooted in the Mass Contact Exercise. Key points that enabled this incredible story include:

- The sheer longevity of the program, institutionalised in 2002 and continuing to date, speaks volumes of the constancy of purpose and commitment displayed by management, HR and all stakeholders

- The patience and resilience displayed in the initial phases allowed the forum to evolve from a platform for emotional catharsis to one where problems and solutions were discussed, and successes celebrated in a spirit of collective ownership and accountability

- This is also a classic case of managing unions and identifying common ground to engage and take all organisational stakeholders on board.

Lessons for Change Managers

The SAIL RSP story is replete with lessons for the discerning change manager. The following are some of most compelling ones we came across:

- No person-dependent movement can sustain itself to reap long-term benefits, even though individual efforts at different points in time form key pieces of the picture. The institutionalization of the larger change theme is necessary for continuity and resilience against changes in personnel, short-term urgencies, etc. This institutionalization requires focused communications and the usage of different reinforcement mechanisms (symbols, aligned people processes, etc.).

- Not every step of the change intervention can be 'driven'. Very often change managers and leaders fall in the trap of trying to curate every stage of the change, stifling the space required for the change to seep in the environment to adapt organically. The manner in which the SAIL RSP management allowed the discussions of the Mass Contact Exercise to evolve and mature over time, not only enhanced employee buy-in, but also helped build the trust critical for meaningful change to follow.

- A meaningfully crafted, effectively communicated vision/mission statement can go beyond the pages of glossy documents and help galvanise the entire organisation towards critical focus areas.

PACT FOR CHANGE

The Tata Motors Story

"Without change there is
no innovation, creativity or
incentive for improvement.
Those who initiate change
will have a better opportunity
to manage the change that is
inevitable."

—Winston Churchill

TATA MOTORS

COMPANY PROFILE

Tata Motors Limited (TML), a flagship company of the Tata Group, is India's largest automobile company with consolidated revenues of $34.7 billion in 2012–13. It is the leader in commercial vehicles in each segment in India and has a strong presence in passenger vehicles with winning products in the compact, midsize car and utility vehicle segments. Over eight million Tata vehicles ply on Indian roads, since the first one rolled out in 1954. The foundation of the company's growth is a deep understanding of economic stimuli and customer needs and the ability to translate them into customer-desired offerings through leading edge R&D.

In the past decade, Tata Motors, the first engineering company from India to be listed on the New York Stock Exchange (September 2004), has emerged as an international automobile company. Through subsidiaries and associate companies, it has operations in the UK, South Korea, Thailand, Spain and South Africa. Among them is Jaguar Land Rover, comprising the two iconic British brands acquired in 2008.

Tata Motors is committed to Corporate Social Responsibility and improving the quality of life of communities by working on four thrust areas—employability, education, health and environment. The activities touch the lives of more than a million citizens. With the foundation of its rich heritage, Tata Motors today is etching a refulgent future.

TML IN AN INCREASINGLY COMPETITIVE BUSINESS ENVIRONMENT

In 2011, the preeminent position held by Tata Motors in commercial vehicles and its hard-earned foothold in passenger vehicles, were increasingly under threat with a host of global automotive giants venturing into the lucrative Indian markets. For Tata Motors to sustain and improve its market position, it needed to establish a culture that encouraged ownership and innovation, raising the bar on performance and responsiveness.

It was evident that such a transformation would need to be rooted in real, ground-level mindset change in employees across levels, supported with the requisite processes and structures.

Introspecting for key focus areas

Operating in the hyper-competitive automotive market, particularly Passenger Vehicles, Tata Motors had always believed in the need to adapt to the dynamics of the business environment the years 2010–11 had already witnessed a series of concerted steps aimed at sustaining and enhancing business performance, addressing pain-points and creating value in the areas of Supply Chain, Quality, Safety, Operations, among others.

One common thread underpinning all of these diverse initiatives, which would serve as Rule #1 was that any successful initiative stood on the binding forces of leadership, together with the driving force of people.

The Tata Motors HR Vision reads, *'To make Tata Motors a world-class destination for best-in-class talent to sustain its business success'*. Driven by this vision, the focus of every HR initiative remains to enable performance and making the environment conducive for the very best talent, so as to drive business performance forward. Key among these was the Gallup Employee Engagement survey, conducted since 2005, enabling Tata Motors to keep track of the organisational pulse across locations, business units and levels.

Performance Measurement and Rewards had always been seen as an integral part of the foundation to build an engaged, productive workforce; a fact which Gallup further underlined. Thus the dip observed in engagement scores on this key driver was a significant area of concern. November 2011 saw HR leaders formally identify 'Performance and Rewards' as a critical focus area to drive employee engagement, with an awareness that it must, as any process or policy, be aligned to the current business and organisational realities.

ENVISIONING THE DESIRED PERFORMANCE MANAGEMENT SYSTEM

While the Employee Engagement journey so far had resulted in significant headway with Action Planning Workshops and team-level interventions to enhance engagement, motivation and commitment, the task of redesigning the Performance & Rewards mechanism was certainly more complex.

It was decided that this pain point would be approached holistically, considering both management and employee perspectives. The following key management perspectives emerged from the diagnostic:

- The Performance Management System (PMS) must elicit greater ownership from employees on goals defined in line with strategy

- Greater accountability for business results

- Strong inter-linkages of goals in a matrix environment to ensure collective ownership

- Adequate stretch in goals

- Compensation structure must be reflective of both individual and organisational performance

To the team's surprise, data collected from employees also reflected similar needs, though with visible deficits in the perceived fairness of the existing system and its ability to distinguish between good and poor performance. This process was aided by the add-on questions inserted by the organisation over and above the Gallup Q12.

The findings from these detailed diagnostics were discussed at length in the Management Committee (ManCom), chaired by the Managing Director, Mr P.M Telang and his management team, comprising leadership from various Business Units and functions.. After much discussion and deliberation, it was decided to reform the existing PMS—and to have the ManCom own the change process was the most important step towards ensuring subsequent adoption and buy-in across levels.

To set the ball rolling on this massive change agenda, a communication from the MD was sent out to all employees as an early assurance that their feedback was valuable and being taken up for action. It was decided to engage Mercer Consulting at this stage, in order to draw on global best practices while also introducing the much needed outside-in perspective on things. Mercer was selected after a rigorous evaluation process and were engaged basis their experience, exposure to benchmark data, global practices and the required bandwidth to cover an organisation as large as Tata Motors.

Working together with Mercer, targeted efforts were made to gather further inputs from employees on the different aspects of the system requiring reform. *Parivartan* (Change), an online listening post was created for employees to share their comments, feedback, and suggestions on the existing system as well as the new system to be conceptualised. Additionally, with a view to pin-point specific areas of dissatisfaction, an online survey was also launched, covering all the stages of the Performance Management System (PMS) from Goal Setting to final Performance Rating.

The feedback indicated that only forty to fifty per cent of the organisation was deploying the goal setting process in the spirit required for effectiveness, linking individual goals with functional and larger organisational imperatives. Most importantly, it was found that meaningful performance discussions was missing in most cases.

The detailed diagnostics and interactions resulted in clarity on the essentials that needed to be incorporated in the new PMS:

- Working to maintain the commitment and active participation of senior leadership and top executives
- Focusing on the right performance measures
- Holding managers accountable for performance feedback and differentiation
- Providing necessary communication and training to effect the change

PACT—FROM IDEATION TO IMPLEMENTATION

The sponsorship obtained from the ManCom early in the game ensured that the entire change intervention was owned by senior leadership, which would prove crucial for buy-in and adoption. Through in-depth discussions with the ManCom on the detailed diagnostics and the desired Performance and Rewards system thereof, evolved **PACT**, i.e. the **Performance**

Assessment and Coaching Tool, the evolved avatar of the PMS at Tata Motors, which held Coaching Discussions at its core. It was clear both to the leaders and the HR Team that this was an opportunity not just to overhaul an aged process, but to build and reinforce a culture that would promote meritocracy and performance.

PACT Philosophy and Spirit

To help clarify and standardise the Performance & Rewards experience across the organisation and also to bring in the required ethic and rigour as an integral part of the ground-level process, core values underlying the Performance Management System were outlined for the first time. This was also important to help establish a common culture of performance delivery and rewards across locations and business units.

i.   **Building Trust**: Eliminating fear and suspicion as operating principles

ii. **Raising the Bar**: Raising one's goals, standards and expectations

iii. **Taking Ownership**: Taking full ownership of any job you do

iv. **Redefining Performance**: Articulating what is required of the system in general, and of individuals in particular

v.   **Aligning Goals**: Ensuring clear understanding of the bigger picture

vi. **Coaching Conversations**: Facilitating a structured dialogue that begins with a sharp focus and ends with the coach stating the agreed actions in their own language

PACT Design

The above values were integrated into the system across the three broad stages of the Performance & Rewards process:

i. **Performance Planning**: Linking individual performance with organisational goals through a meaningful dialogue focusing on micro (individual) and macro level (organisational) imperatives

ii. **Performance Review & Feedback**: Holding coaching conversations, providing feedback on strengths and developmental areas, propagating a culture of trust and transparency

iii. **Performance Rewards & Capability Development**: In order to drive forward a performance culture with greater clarity on rewards' linkages to delivered performance, PACT introduced a performance measurement mechanism that clearly defined performance levels and behavioural expectations, enabling commensurate rewards thereafter. Corporate performance was also factored into this system, with the relative weightage increasing with seniority in the organisational hierarchy.

Additionally, PACT was designed to strengthen the spirit of development and performance enhancement, by linking employees' Individual Learning Plans (on PACT), with the Learning Management System (LMS) managed by the Learning & Development team. This focus on development as a means of enhancing performance was further augmented with career planning discussions.

PACT incorporated a series of mechanisms to help focus performance better and enhance the overall effectiveness of the system:

i. Stronger alignment, with Business Unit (BU) and Functional Heads aligning goals first at business level and the cascade process for driving the same down the line.

ii. Greater focus and accountability, the number of goals was limited to a maximum of nine, thus avoiding dilution of focus and energies.

iii. A classification of goals as Strategic (BU level imperatives), Tactical (department level) and Individual (individual employee level) was introduced, to enable employees to focus their energies as required by their roles in the organisation.

iv. The erstwhile Performance Rating scale (six-point) was replaced by a crisper, more meaningful, comprehensively defined four-level scale. This was done as the previous scale was found to be underutilised and lacking in uniform interpretation.

v. Greater transparency around normalisation of ratings, with figures being finalised by Performance Apex Committees (PACs) with inputs from Managers and then communicated to employees. This helped to not only enhance transparency, but also underline the fact that final ratings and the normalization process were owned by the Business and not HR.

vi. Cohort-based Normalization: With a view to avoid the concentration

PACT Rating Scale*

All appraisees will be rated on a 4 point scale. A description of each of the scale points is provided below:

Exceptional Contribution	Strong Contribution	Satisfactory Contribution	Contribution Needs Improvement
• Performance Far Exceeds objectives	• Performance Exceeds objectives	• Performance Meets objectives	• Performance meets objectives only partially
• Consistently displays top performance in own peer group and across situations	• Comes close to a top performer in the peer group	• Consistently solid and delivers on expectations	• Often fails to meet performance objectives - quality, quantity, cost, timelines
• Always raises the bar for self and team	• Often raises the bar for self and team	• Rarely sets new performance benchmarks	• Comfortable accepting mediocrity
• Demonstrates deep expertise and a "take charge" approach for delivering high impact results	• Demonstrates above average expertise and takes ownership of self/team results	• Demonstrates acceptable functional proficiency and takes ownership of results in most situations	• Displays unsatisfactory functional proficiency of skills and only occasionally takes ownership of results
• Displays outstanding people skills to successfully influence stakeholders	• Displays strong interpersonal skills and builds relations beyond the immediate work group	• Displays acceptable interpersonal skills; gets along with most team members	• Displays poor interpersonal skills; is seen as somebody difficult to work with
• Always connects own/team goals to the larger strategic aspirations of the organization	• Often displays awareness of Org context and factors in the same in own area of work	• Displays fair awareness of the larger organization context but may not always be able to connect own goals to the same	• Largely unaware of the organization context of one's work
• Has a strong sense of urgency about anticipating and resolving explicit and unstated problems	• Displays fair initiative to take on additional responsibilities, beyond immediate area of work	• Displays fair initiative but largely is restricted to one's immediate area of work	• Slow to take initiative and accept responsibility for own work
• Displays inspirational role model leadership; exhibits high impact team building/mentoring skills	• Encourages diverse perspectives, gives honest and constructive feedback, reinforces team for their contribution	• Participates in team situations, shares and receives developmental feedback and works on it	• Displays low team involvement in work situations
• Prioritizes naturally; always makes apt and speedy decisions	• Invests fair time to coach team members; ensures talent pipeline development	• Open to different points of view, offers support for other's ideas	• Displays lack of interest in team engagement and development
• Always exhibits a "customer delight" mindset – anticipating and delivering breakthrough solutions	• Is comfortable prioritizing; mostly makes fair and quick decisions	• With some help, can make decisions in time	• Decision making is typically slow and reactive
• Consistently demonstrates passion for new learning with an "outside in" bias	• Consistently demonstrates a "customer first" mindset in all areas of work	• Engages with customers and usually responds to their expectations	• Does not proactively engage with the customer to understand expectations
	• Proactively seeks opportunities to learn beyond the routine	• Positively responds to learning opportunities	• Indifferent to new learning

*This guide is meant to be illustrative and not exhaustive. Appraisers are expected to take a holistic view of the appraisee's quantum of performance, the context of performance, behaviors underlying the performance and the relativity of performance with relevant peer group in the specific appraisal year while deciding on the overall rating.

of higher ratings at senior levels PACT ensured that the normalization process was conducted among peer-level employees only.

SPREADING THE WORD ON PACT!

With the ManCom having finalised on the PACT process design in October 2011 and with the system set to go-live with the Mid-Term and Final Performance Reviews for 2011–12, the communication and process adoption challenge was immense, especially considering the targeted employee base was approx. 14,000, spread across six plant locations and nearly forty commercial teams. A detailed launch process was embarked upon:

i. **Central Launch**, by Mr P.M Telang (Managing Director, Tata Motors) and Mr Prabir Jha (Chief Human Resources Officer), Performance & Rewards Team, and Mercer Team: This was targeted at senior management from across units and locations and helped resolve queries and ambiguities, to ensure greater acceptance and ownership at the top levels.

ii. **Location-wise Launches**, owned by the Business Unit Head and Head—HR at respective locations: This targeted the Executive Grade employees across locations. With HR's messaging on the new process and system accompanied by detailed context setting by senior leadership, this phase helped prepare the environment for the large-scale deployment to follow.

iii. **Town Halls**, owned by Functional Heads, HR and PACT Teams: This was the last leg of the communication and orientation exercise, and entailed up to three sessions being conducted at every location, with standardised communication and messaging.

These concerted steps not only helped communicate the essential features of the new system, but also helped clarify just how it would impact the working lives of employees and what were the performance and behavioural expectations from employees moving forward. At every step, active feedback was encouraged to help address concerns early in the game and ensure a smooth and effective transition to the new system.

BUILDING MOMENTUM TO WIN OVER NAYSAYERS

Driving change against the natural forces of resistance and organisational inertia requires proactive measures to be thought of and put in place. For PACT therefore, change ambassadors were identified and trained, using the 'Train the Trainer' (TTT) format, to enable them to orient employees and address queries down the line. These day-long TTTs covered roughly twenty to twenty-five per cent of the senior executives at every location, from HR, line and PACT Teams.

These trainers then conducted PACT Training sessions for appraisers, covering eighty-seven per cent of the population over two months. These sessions focused on sensitising Appraisers on the need for change, enhancing awareness on the various changes in the new system, including the linkage to promotions (thus discouraging tenure-based movements) and driving a culture of coaching conversations.

The different phases of the process, including the Clarificatory Discussion, Normalisation with PACs and sharing of ratings and feedback were concluded within planned timelines and in a manner that highlighted the transparent nature of the new system. This helped build momentum and drive process adoption thereon. Findings from the Annual PMS Survey further validated these positive feelers.

EMBEDDING PACT INTO THE ORGANISATIONAL FABRIC

The early, hard-earned wins paved the way for efforts towards truly institutionalising the new system. The first step in this regard was the Goal Setting exercise for the year. The process enabled the cascade and alignment of goals across functions, starting with the Business Unit Scorecard.

A strong Plan-Do-Check-Act (PDCA) mechanism helped govern the implementation of the processes, reflecting a strong lessons-learnt orientation, drawing on 'Things gone right' and 'Things gone wrong' from the previous year's process implementation. Key measures adopted include:

i.   At the beginning of any process cycle (Goal Setting/ Mid Year Review/ Final Performance Review), all Appraisers were required to share a calendar for PACT discussions covering all relevant employees.

ii.   With this line of sight available in advance, the HR would send a reminder SMS to the concerned Appraiser and employee on the scheduled date.

iii. This was followed by a confirmation call the next day; in case the discussion could not take place, it was formally rescheduled to a later date.

> "PACT is a tool of the business since it was co-created by the Leadership Team of Tata Motors. To my mind, the most significant improvements PACT has brought about is in the way we administer the performance management system and in the way we particularly set our goals. The system encourages a discussion on goals and critically focuses on documentation of goals in the online system which has brought in a culture of transparency and accountability."
>
> —Girish Wagh, Head PPPM, Passenger Vehicle Business Unit, Tata Motors

This systematic drive and rigour helped raise PACT discussion coverage rates to ninety-seven-per cent, which has been the single-most powerful driver of the system's success. Additionally, for the first time in the organisation's history, employees receiving a 'Contribution Needs Improvement' rating were empanelled on to a Performance Improvement Plan.

In several cases it was observed that Managers, in spite of making earnest attempts at having meaningful discussions with their employees, were still unable to do so. Targeting this crucial competency gap, a module titled 'Coaching ImPACT' was launched in December 2012. This module included People Managers across locations and units. A 'New First Line Manager' module was also deployed in February 2013, aimed at holistically developing first-time people managers on key capabilities crucial for fostering a healthy team ethic and high performance culture.

Active communications continue to form the backbone of PACT efforts, with Business leaders and HR endorsing the fact that one iteration never guarantees real adoption and institutionalization.

This chapter is based on the entry submitted by Prabir Jha (Sr. Vice President & CHRO—Tata Motors Ltd.), Vineet Soni (Head—Performance and Rewards, Tata Motors Ltd.) at the Best Change Interventions of Asia Study 2012

What Tata Motors did differently to successfully manage and drive change

The PACT design and implementation at Tata Motors demonstrates distinctive efforts in successful change design, roll-out and adoption:

- The relentless focus on listening to and acting on the voice of employees at different stages of the process—from identifying lacunas in the previous system, to the design of the ideal system in the current business scenario, to scanning for pain-points in the new system. This rigour and commitment helped win the trust and confidence of employees, thus enhancing buy-in and early momentum for the change.

- Identifying and communicating the values espoused by the new Performance Management System served to clarify exactly what PACT stood for and how the Management saw it contributing to a more transparent, equitable, performance oriented culture and enhanced business results thereon.

Lessons for Change Managers

The Tata Motors story presents vital insights on how a large, geographically dispersed organisation can drive and attempt to institutionalise change, overcoming major challenges of scale and process standardization among other challenges:

- The successful execution of the structured, phase-wise launch—Central à Location-wise Town Halls—goes way beyond charting out a neat Project Plan document. Ensuring key stakeholders and influencers are on board and maintaining consistent and coherent communications are among the several building blocks that need to be in place to drive change successfully.

- Taking customers on board early in the game not only enhances buy-in and adoption, but also helps refine and validate the defined change.

- Lastly and relating perhaps to the single weakest link along the Change Management path, institutionalising the change requires a lot of hard work and rigour across levels, for the hallowed shifts in culture and organisational mindset to really come about. Changes in the 'soft stuff' require some serious efforts in terms of the 'hard stuff'. So while the start is good—change efforts need to be sustained to succeed.

LEARNING BY DOING WAR ROOM PROJECTS

The Wartsila Story

"It's not that some people have willpower and some don't... It's that some people are ready to change and others are not"

—James Gordon

CREATING AN URGENCY AROUND A VISION FOR CHANGE

The year 2012 was characterised by an uncertain global economic environment with GDP growth rates slowing down from 3.8per cent to 3.3 per cent, this was accentuated by a nose dive in availability of domestic gas and ever-increasing Heavy Fuel Oil (HFO) prices leading to decreased profitability for power plant and ship owners.

In India the Central Electricity Authority (CEA) announced that no new gas-based power plant would be set up in the country till 2015–16. Economists predicted that this would lead to a thirty-fiveper cent fall in India's natural gas production in 2012–13 and could further dip by twelve per cent in 2013–14. This would in particular adversely affect the Indian power producers (some of whom where existing clients of Wartsila) who had commissioned their plant but were unable to initiate operations due to non-availability of gas.

In view of the uncertain Business environment, the Management of Wartsila realised that while individual business units were passionately pursuing a growth strategy a concerted effort needed to be undertaken by all to reduce the cost of goods sold (COGS). This was based on the simple thumb rule that if the COGS was reduced accompanied by a one per cent increase in sale price, there would be a double digit increase in EBIT (Earnings Before Interest and Tax) margins for Wartsila which would have a positive impact on the bottom line.

The Management conceptualised a change initiative called the **War Room** to bring down the cost of goods sold. This would lead to optimised resources, material and processes, challenge the existing status-quo, support the selling teams by providing cost competitiveness and ensure overall profitability of operations.

The War Room code was conceptualised after extensive discussions and debates between the Management Team (SteCo), Senior Leaders, Key Influencers and the high potential young leaders (Gen X) of the organisation. The collective realisation was to develop a proactive and innovative approach for driving performance, convert challenges into opportunities and maintain customer focus while delivering on existing quality standards.

OPERATIONALISING THE CHANGE

Accordingly eighteen Bring Down Cost (BDC) projects were initiated in April 2012 with two additional projects being added midway, under the umbrella of the War Room intervention. All twenty War Room projects were to be run as 'Companies' by identified employees who were assigned different managerial roles. Each company was given a fictional valuation of ten million Indian rupees (USD 161,000) with its own CEO, Leadership Teams and Managerial cadre. The CEO and Management for these twenty War Room companies constituted of seventy-two cross-functional and cross-hierarchical employees who were responsible for steering and managing their respective companies. All twenty companies were mentored by the Wartsila India Management team who took active interest in monitoring their progress.

Each War Room company CEO had to upload basic details of their project, the company charter and progress with regards achievement of specific milestones on a monthly basis on the internal knowledge management portal at Wartsila—Integrated Document Management (IDM). Basis this information, each company was reviewed and rated by a pool of 350 Managers on a point scale of one(low) to seven(high). The points received depicted the rater's perception about each company's performance against the stated purpose and assigned targets. The ratings were based on *Performance* (Was the target challenging?, did the results reflect sustainable performance?, comparison with industry benchmarks etc) and *Approach* (Whether the approach was appropriate, clear and well defined?, whether the practices used were innovative, improving the process and supporting targets). At the end of three months all companies were audited and a sustainable plan of action was to be formulated at the end of six months re-emphasising the Management's commitment towards sustaining the positive impact of the initiative.

The change interventions served two major purposes—a) it made employees accountable for the success of the Company and embedded the entrepreneurial spirit of achieving excellence b) it brought to the forefront many innovative ideas for bringing down cost through sharing of ideas and monthly evaluations.

DESIGNING A COMMUNICATION STRATEGY AND ENSURING SOUND FEEDBACK MECHANISMS

A monthly newsletter BDC Times was published summarising the progress of each War Room company. The newsletter featured overall progress of each company with a CEO message / interview and recognised the top three companies (in terms of valuation)for their excellent work.

Mr Rakesh Sarin, the Managing Director of Wartsila in particular, took keen interest in motivating the BDC companies through monthly communications encouraging them to continually raise the bar on performance. All the BDC companies were also showcased during the Wartsila Growth Conclaves which were organised every quarter across India.

Key insights from the BDC initiative were integrated and made part of a learning intervention aimed at covering a critical mass of around three hundred employees. This was very successful in aligning key influencers on the need for the change intervention and also for securing their buy-in.

In addition, relevant information on all the twenty projects was made available on the Wartsila Intranet (Compass) which could be accessed by all employees in India across locations.

MANAGING INITIAL RESISTANCE, LEVERAGING EARLY WINS AND INSTITUTIONALISING THE CHANGE

The Management Team at Wartsila kept a close track on the progress of each company by mentoring individual projects. All Wartsila employees could view progress on milestones set and were encouraged by Mr Rakesh Sarin (the Managing Director) to provide their valuable input even if they were not assigned formal reviewer roles.

A customised learning intervention was conceptualised for key stakeholders (Critical Talent—about thirty percent of the population) with the primary objective of securing their buy-in and sharing ideas and trigger discussions on enhancing effectiveness of the Change Interventions.

Companies whose valuations had increased substantially were showcased to the larger group of employees establishing a Lessons Learnt Culture, a key determining trait of learning organisations.

A detailed audit was also conducted three months post initiation of the change intervention to bring in greater focus on how individual companies were managed. The audits provided the management with

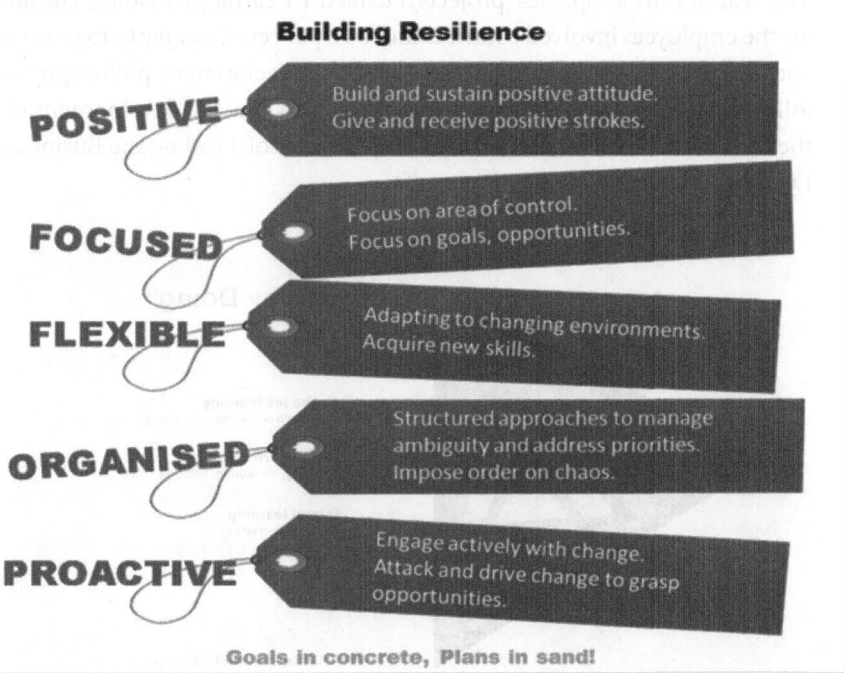

Building Resilience

POSITIVE — Build and sustain positive attitude. Give and receive positive strokes.

FOCUSED — Focus on area of control. Focus on goals, opportunities.

FLEXIBLE — Adapting to changing environments. Acquire new skills.

ORGANISED — Structured approaches to manage ambiguity and address priorities. Impose order on chaos.

PROACTIVE — Engage actively with change. Attack and drive change to grasp opportunities.

Goals in concrete, Plans in sand!

an objective assessment of the valuations of individual companies (an outcome of the ratings received). The audits particularly focussed on results achieved by the company in the course of three months with specific comments on how performance could be further bettered upon. The final outcome of the audit was an 'Overall Assurance Rating' for each company, based on several pre-determined parameters which were published internally for the reference of employees assigned reviewer roles.

At the end of six months, the continuation phase commenced to ensure that benefits achieved were sustainable and not just 'a one-time blip' and to build structures and processes to sustain potential benefits accruing in the medium to long run. The CEOs of the War Room Companies and their teams had to put in specific systems and processes to ensure sustainability of efficiency and improved productivity achieved in the first six months. This gradually became the 'new normal' and an integral part of the Wartsila way of working.

IMPACT ON THE ORGANISATION

The War Room Companies (projects) enabled a 'Learning by Doing' culture for the employees involved contributing to 70 per cent *Learning by Experience* and 20 per cent by *Mentoring* (the 70–20–10 development philosophy is followed at Wartsila). The BDC experience also enabled development of the three core Warstila Leadership competencies of Leading the Business, Leading People and Delivering results.

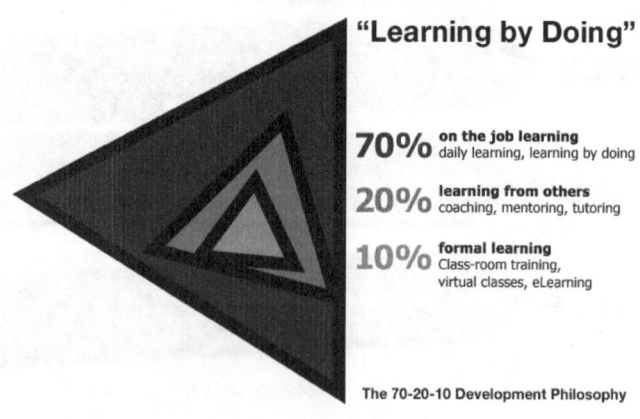

"Learning by Doing"

70% on the job learning
daily learning, learning by doing

20% learning from others
coaching, mentoring, tutoring

10% formal learning
Class-room training,
virtual classes, eLearning

The 70-20-10 Development Philosophy

Proactive participation of the larger population of employees for reviewing monthly progress of key milestones for individual projects was the key for realising the full potential of each project and ensuring optimal 'learning on the job' for the participants. This also enabled alignment of employees with Wartsila's global focus on the 'Entrepreneurial way of working' in an extremely challenging business environment. The outcomes of these innovative solutions generated by the CEOs and the management teams of the War Room Teams led to concrete money saving in the immediate term and enhanced overall operational productivity for the long term sustenance of operations.

> "Keeping the Organisation in high spirits, motivated and challenged, especially in tough times, is of paramount importance. This need was felt by the Management Team and to fulfil this objective, the principles of the War Room to *Bring Down the Cost of Goods Sold* were set up. As is evident from the outcome of this initiative, the softer objective were achieved to a high level of satisfaction and on top of it, this exercise yielded important financial rewards."
>
> —*Rakesh Sarin, MD—Wartsila India Ltd*

All the employees at Wartsila experienced a high-energy, action-packed six months post kick-off of the War Room projects. The enthusiasm and excitement of the CEOs of the BDC companies and their management teams for successful deployment and completion of the company's charter was contagious.

In the first six months of operations, the twenty War Room companies contributed to twenty-fiveper cent of the EBIT for Wartsila in 2012. The BDC teams worked together, challenged the status quo and ensured timely realization of assigned milestones. Some of the teams even exceeded their self-stated goals by implementing innovative solutions re-establishing their commitment for achieving business results.

The Sustainability phase was initiated on completion of the first six months of setting up of the companies with the CEOs and their teams putting together systems and processes in place to ensure continued efficiency and productivity. The CEOs were entrusted with the task of periodically monitoring performance of assigned companies and recording the long-term benefits accrued. This included announcing the company charter and documenting estimated benefits for the company in the next three years as part of Phase II.

The assessment of Phase II was made by the Wartsila Management on the basis of the company charter, milestones achieved and long/medium term sustainability of the benefits achieved. The winners were announced in the presence of the global CEO of Wartsila and a large gathering of leaders and employees. The War Room Teams were awarded for their exemplary contributions and were recognised for re-establishing Wartsila's vision of being the most valued business partner for their customers by creating better technologies, benefitting both the customer as well as the environment.

This chapter is based on the entry submitted by Usha Venkatesh (AVP-HR, Wartsila India Ltd.) at the Best Change Interventions of Asia Study 2012

What Wartsila did differently to successfully manage and drive change

In view of the uncertain global economic environment, characterised by slowdown in growth rates and ever increasing input prices, Wartsila undertook a concerted effort to bring down the Cost of Goods Sold (COGS) which would automatically impact the bottom line by increasing the EBIT margins. Accordingly the management conceptualised a change initiative called the War Room to achieve optimised resources, bring down the cost of goods sold and ensure overall profitability of operations.

- The War Room code was conceptualised post extensive discussions and debates between key stakeholders including Leaders, Management Teams, Key Influencers and High Potential Young Leaders.

- Twenty Action Learning Projects (christened War Room Projects) were initiated under the aegis of the War Room initiative, with each project being positioned as a separate company with its own Leadership Teams and a fictional valuation of ten million INR (USD 161,000).

- Each War Room Project CEO had to periodically update progress against set milestones on a monthly basis which was reviewed by a pool of over three hundred and fifty Managers. The ratings received in turn impacted the company's valuation.

- Each project was closely tracked by the Wartsila management and success stories were periodically shared across the organisations to build a Best Practices and a 'Lessons Learnt' culture.

- Detailed audits were conducted three months post initialization of each project to provide an objective assessment of the valuations of each company and provided structured inputs for further improvement of performance.

- At the end of six months, the leadership teams of War Room Projects had to put in specific systems and processes to ensure long term sustenance of implemented practices. War Room Projects which had substantially contributed to reduction in cost and increased profitability were also recognised in the presence of the Global CEO of Wartsila.

Lessons for Change Managers

The Wartsila story presents the following key lessons for change managers conceptualising and driving interventions in organisations:

- Identify key success factors for enhanced business performance and design the change intervention around these themes.

- Empower individuals and teams by assigning clear roles and make employees accountable for the success of the change intervention.

- Regularly monitor progress of the intervention and create a structured review mechanism for providing periodic inputs/feedback to team members.

- Ensure percolation of success stories / innovative ideas arising from the change intervention through regular communication building a 'Lessons Learnt' culture across the organisation.

- Institutionalise support systems/ processes to ensure that benefits accrued from the intervention are sustained in the medium/ long run contributing to enhanced business performance.

TRANSCEND: Building Leaders for Tomorrow

The Wipro Story

"It doesn't matter where you are,
you are nowhere compared to
where you can go."

—Bob Proctor

CREATING AN URGENCY AROUND A VISION FOR CHANGE

As a global information technology, consulting and outsourcing company, Wipro helps its customers manage their businesses better by leveraging its industry-wide experience, deep technological expertise, comprehensive portfolio of services and vertically aligned business model.

> "The landscape of opportunities in the domains of Manufacturing & Hi Tech (Mfg-Hitech) is fast changing. The impact of effective leadership pipeline will be far reaching in capturing these vast opportunities and it is very clear that in order to stay ahead of the industry we need a paradigm shift in the way we operate. We need to move from being just a vendor to a trusted partner. This requires a change in the mindset of our employees, especially the leaders."
>
> —NS Bala, Sr. Vice President & Global Head, Manufacturing and Hi Tech SBU, Wipro

The Manufacturing and Hi Tech Strategic Business Unit (SBU) is the second largest business unit at Wipro with a revenue size of more than USD one billion. The SBU had successfully pursued aggressive growth targets over the fiscal 2009–2011 and had been performing remarkably well in an otherwise volatile Information Technology space. This remarkable growth story was an outcome of the persistent efforts of the leadership team of the Manufacturing & Hi-Tech SBU who recognised the need for the Business Unit to be perceived as a strategic business partner so it could leverage competitive advantages in an otherwise uncertain business environment. The Wipro management therefore prioritised the institutionalization of a structured Leadership Development Intervention at the SBU level . This

intervention would focus on building a robust talent pipeline and an agile talent pool of competent senior level managers who would lead the organisation to greater heights. This led to the conceptualization and roll-out of the 'Transcend—Building Leaders for Tomorrow' Program.

OPERATIONALISING THE CHANGE

The 'Transcend' program was institutionalised with the primary objective of developing a pool of senior level managers who would mirror Wipro Leadership Qualities and facilitate the process of the SBU being perceived as a strategic business partner creating value for its stakeholders.

One of the key elements of the Transcend initiative was to identify and articulate characteristics that determine the leadership effectiveness in the context of the Hi Tech SBU and the organisation at large. These qualities, termed as Wipro Leadership Qualities were arrived at after much research and reflection, and were articulated to establish a clear connect between Wipro's strategic drivers and the role leaders played in making these come alive.

The program therefore aimed at

- Building a culture of client centricity whereby leaders would take ownership for the success/ failure of the client's endeavour and create win-win partnerships with zeal.

- Providing a strategic perspective on the macro and micro implications of the need for this change intervention.

- Creating execution savvy and result oriented leaders who would handle obstacles and challenges associated with change and risk management and would turn ideas into reality by staying focussed on identified business goals through their strategic perspective.

- Enabling a nurturing environment and encouraging collaborative working.

The figure below displays the six Wipro Leadership Qualities, which would serve as the backbone of the Transcend Leadership Development Intervention. All subsequent actionables defined as part of the delivery and execution of Transcend were articulated basis the following six qualities.

The program commenced with identification of participants, mostly high performing, high potential employees of the manufacturing and Hi-tech SBU who were incumbents/successors of key critical roles. The performance-potential categorization was done basis actual performance ratings documented in the previous two years and outcomes of 360 degree feedback sessions were used to determine potential to take on higher roles. Designed as a year-long intervention, Transcend commenced in August 2012 with forty leaders being identified as part of the target population. To maximise the benefit of this learning intervention, Wipro chose the DDI 70–20–10 principle of learning model. The idea was to enable seventy per cent of learning through 'On the Job' assignments also called 'Bubble assignments', twenty per cent through 'Coaching and ten per cent through customised training interventions.

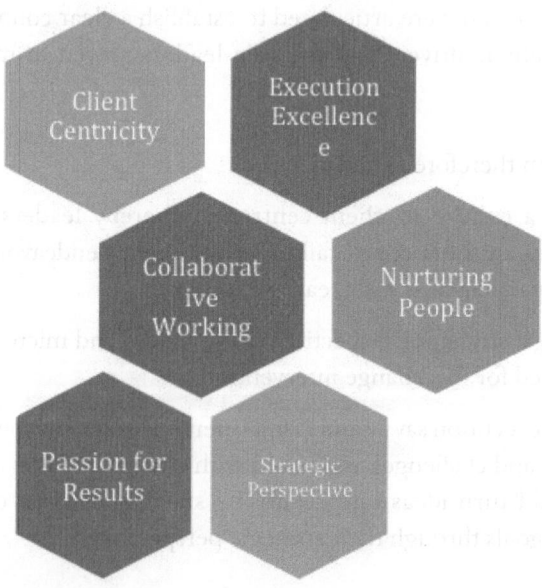

Each Transcend participant was assigned a mentor—usually a senior leader from Wipro from the same function but belonging to a different business vertical. Each mentor was assigned two to three Transcend participants with mentor-mentee meetings scheduled at least once every quarter. Formal and informal mentor-mentee meetings and leadership connect meets were organised throughout the year to ensure alignment of mentors and Transcend participants.

The **Mentoring Conversations** facilitated the process of supportive inquiry that addressed the strengths and developmental areas of the Transcend participants while simultaneously linking back to larger organisational goals. This also served the added purpose of securing senior management buy-in into the initiative by involving key stakeholders right from design to the execution phase.

To meet SBU-specific needs, several interviews were conducted with the leadership team, mentors and program participants to get a detailed overview of the prevailing business context, understand program expectations and identify development gaps (of participants).

This subsequently led to the creation of customised **Individual Development Plans** for the Transcend participant in consultation with his/her manager and mentor. This was based on the past performance of the participant, 360 degree competency assessment and predicted future role requirements.

Development areas were identified for each participant based on the feedback received in the 360-degree feedback survey and performance appraisal. IDP discussions helped in building a personalised connect with each participant and also helped them understand the value they could derive from the program.

Customised training programs and knowledge sharing sessions were conducted once in two months to bridge identified competency gaps and provide a platform for enhanced greater bonding among participants from various locations and functions.

In addition to this, articles and executive summaries from eminent publications on core technical/ functional areas were periodically shared with participants under the aegis of the **Learning Window**

Series. Regular leadership connects were organised between the participants and the SBU Head / members of the leadership team re-enforcing the commitment of management in developing the capabilities of the Transcend participants.

A distinctive feature of the Transcend intervention were **Action Learning Projects (termed Bubble Assignments)** under which a team of five to six Transcend participants would work on a real life business problem and propose an executable solution which would help the SBU's objectives.

The members of each Bubble Assignment team were identified basis their skills, experience and areas of interest. Each Bubble Assignment had a sponsor, champion (Project team leader) and team members. The sponsor was usually a senior leader / subject matter expert whose primary responsibility was to mentor the project and thereby give direction and focus to the project team. The projects assigned were often an outcome of the strategic drivers crafted at the organisation level and were mentored by a senior leader / subject matter expert from Wipro.

Each Bubble Assignment was institutionalised for a time period of three to four months with periodic monthly reviews and a final project review at the end of the fourth month. The two best Bubble Assignments which had positively impacted realisation of business goals were awarded by the Wipro leadership team.

DESIGNING A COMMUNICATION STRATEGY AND ENSURING SOUND FEEDBACK MECHANISMS

Given that the Transcend program was a year-long initiative it was imperative that Wipro undertook a structured communication campaign to ensure momentum and positive energies associated with this intervention was sustained throughout the year. A well-defined communication campaign was also required to secure buy-in of key stakeholders and keep participants motivated throughout the duration of Transcend.

To emphasise that Transcend was a business driven initiative, the first communication of the program was sent by the SBU head to individual participants. This was followed by a personalised communication to participants from the BU head detailing the outline of the year long program. Subsequently a detailed orientation was provided to the Transcend participants by the Business Unit (BU) HR head—to communicate the objective & relevance of the program and set expectations.

In addition, formal channels of communication like the internet, teleconferences, face to face meetings were extensively used to periodically report out the progress of the Transcend program to key stakeholders. This helped sustain and re-enforce the positive energies built by the program.

MANAGING INITIAL RESISTANCE, LEVERAGING EARLY WINS AND INSTITUTIONALISING THE CHANGE

The greatest challenge faced by the Transcend team was to secure the buy-in of the leadership team and build the program credibility by enabling participants to bridge observed skill-gaps. Given that the program demanded a significant investment from both participants as well as their mentors it was imperative that positive energies emerging from the program were sustained and reinforced periodically.

Accordingly a meeting was organised with the program sponsor (the SBU head) and all his direct reportees (vertical heads / function heads) at the time of program design to make the change intervention robust and ensure that the learning stuck. Their views were also solicited during the definition of the Bubble themes which lead to the identification of key strategic drivers at the organisational level.

The customised training sessions provided a formal launch pad for the Transcend initiative and led to enhanced team synergies and collaboration. This was particularly important given that participants of the program were based across multiple locations and diverse functional areas and many were meeting each other for the very first time.

The Individual Development Plan (IDP) discussions with the participants in presence of the Transcend participant, his/her manager and the HR leader helped build a personalised connect with each participant and reinforced the organisation's commitment towards creating a robust leadership pipeline.

A well-defined Rewards and Recognition framework was conceptualised to sustain motivation levels and address the 'What's in it for Me' (WIIFM) perspective for Transcend participants. Subsequently rewards were announced for the Best Bubble Assignment, Best Mentor, Best Participant and Best Action on the Individual Development Plan. In addition, success stories were also shared across the Business Unit post conclusion of the change intervention substantiating the effectiveness of the Transcend program.

In order to institutionalise the change and ensure that the learning stuck the Transcend team maintained a comprehensive report of each participant (including his IDP, Bubble Assignment details, training program attended etc). This report has become a critical input for the annual talent and succession planning exercise for the Manufacturing and Hi-Tech SBU.

IMPACT ON THE ORGANISATION

Forty middle to senior level managers were directly covered in the Transcend program which has positively impacted the entire workforce of the manufacturing and Hi Tech Business Unit by establishing an incubating culture promoting performance excellence.

The Transcend program has in particular positively impacted customer centricity and execution excellence across the manufacturing and Hi Tech SBU. The SBU Net Perception Score (NPS) (where Transcend was launched) improved from five in 2012 to 22.5 in 2013 with engagement scores increasing to sixty-four per cent with an overwhelming ten per cent increase in employee participation from seventy-four to eighty-four per cent. Quarter IV saw the SBU grow by over 3.2per cent with attrition rates exhibiting a fast declining trend over the past four quarters. This re-established the massive impact that the Transcend initiative has had on the manufacturing and Hi Tech SBU in particular and the entire organisation in general.

While there were other complementary initiatives that possibly contributed to the overall improvements, the Transcend program definitely helped empower managers to lead and prioritise customer centric initiatives thereby creating a pool of Execution Savvy, Result Oriented leaders who were competent in addressing challenges associated with change and risk management in a dynamic global business environment.

This chapter is based on the entry submitted by Sarika Pradhan Jena
(General Manager & Head—HR, Manufacturing & Hi Tech SBU—Wipro Ltd.),
Shveta Srivastava (Manager—HR, Manufacturing & Hi Tech SBU—Wipro Ltd.),
Namitha Shriwastav (Assistant Manager—HR, Manufacturing & Hi Tech SBU—Wipro Ltd.)
at the Best Change Interventions of Asia Study 2012

What Wipro did differently to successfully manage and drive change

The Wipro Hi-Tech SBU institutionalised the Transcend program with the objective of developing a pool of middle to senior level managers who would epitomise the Wipro leadership behaviours and facilitate the process of the SBU becoming a strategic business partner for key stakeholders.

- The initiative was primarily designed to build a strong Leadership pipeline, especially given the strategic positioning of the Hi Tech SBU as one of the organisations largest Business Units.

- The program was extended to include high performing high potential employees and the 70–20–10 principle was adopted to facilitate optimum learning transfer.

- Subject matter experts were assigned as mentors and mentor-mentee meets were periodically organised to create an incubating culture to encourage and nurture talent.

- Customised Individual Development Plans were created for each identified high performing high potential Leader and cutting edge learning resources were periodically shared to build technical/functional capability.

- The progress of individual IDPs was closely tracked by the Wipro management and customised learning interventions were designed to bridge skill-gaps.

- Action Learning Projects (termed Bubble Assignments) were set up to enable the identified talent pool to work on real life business challenges and propose executable solutions

- A well-defined Rewards and Recognition mechanism was conceptualised to sustain and enhance motivation levels.

- The program positively impacted customer centricity and execution excellence and led to higher engagement scores substantially reducing attrition.

Lessons for Change Managers

The Wipro story presents the following key lessons for change managers:

- Building a strong leadership pipeline especially at middle to senior levels is imperative given the nature of business and the uncertainty associated in post-recessionary times. This reinforces the need to conceptualise and design structured Leadership Development Interventions for sustenance of long term milestones.

- Identifying and articulating traits and competencies that determine effectiveness of leaders in the prevailing organisational context is key while designing leadership interventions.

- A clearly defined Rewards and Recognition mechanism is required to reinforce and sustain motivation for contributing to the change efforts.

- Creating a 'Lessons Learnt' culture and percolating success stories across the organisation can build momentum and reinforce key features of the change program.

- The organisational competency framework must be aligned with the design of the intervention to facilitate capability building. Involving senior leaders as subject matter experts/ coaches helps secure buy-in of leadership teams and facilitates creation of an incubating culture promoting nurturing.

- Having clear metrics for assessing effectiveness of leaders post conclusion of the Leadership Development Intervention is key. The Intervention should be looked upon as the starting point and not as the finishing line and must be reinforced and sustained by providing participants continuous learning inputs and feedback going forward.

FREEDOM, ACCOUNTABI- LITY AND A PASSION FOR EXCELLENCE

The Zensar Story

"Whosoever desires constant
success must change his
conduct with the times."

—Niccolo Machiavelli

ZenSar
TECHNOLOGIES
Your Transformation Partner

Zensar Technologies is a technology partner of choice for global organisations looking to strategically transform, grow and lead in today's challenging business environment. Backed by a strong track-record of innovation and over 7,000 associates, it has a global footprint with a presence in more than twenty locations across the world.

PROGRESSIVE CHANGE, BUILDING ON A CULTURE OF PARTICIPATIVE MANAGEMENT

Zensar has been an active advocate and practitioner of the 'Growth by Participative Management' school of thought. This is evident from the success of the Vision Community (VC) initiative, launched in 2001. Through the VC, Zensar offers all employees a voice in building the organisation. The leadership team is committed to fostering an entrepreneurial culture and allowing people to experiment with new ideas, leading to great new products and services. The VC also helps in aligning individual ideas with the organisation's vision and strategy, and spot talent for future business challenges.

With the VC initiative having matured and successfully internalised within the organisation, Zensar sought to take participation to a larger scale, with a directed focus on driving passion, engagement and excellence as a virtuous cycle fuelling individual and organisational goals. Towards this end were born the following dual initiatives, which would be deployed in a phased, concerted manner:

1. **iZen**: Driving Freedom and Accountability as two sides of the same coin, enlisting the participation and endorsement of all Zensar employees with the objective of enhancing engagement

2. **JUGNU**: Driving 'Passion for Excellence' as a lived value across the organisation, bringing every Zensarian together in the shared quest for individual and organisational actualization

MOBILISING THE ORGANISATION TOWARDS A VISION FOR CHANGE

In the beginning of FY 2011 Zensar's Talent Management Committee, comprising Business and HR Heads, decided that the talent management focus for the year would be on instilling higher leadership capabilities in people managers and to consciously drive engagement across the organisation. This was in the context of key innovation triggers identified by this Committee:

- Zensar's ambitious USD One Billion goal by 2016, needed excellent teams, not just excellent individuals

- Zensar's engagement score, traditionally a strength, had decreased consecutively in the previous two years. This was a matter of high concern as engagement impacts both productivity and retention.

- Operating in the service-centric IT / ITES space, non-linear impact was heavily contingent on the engagement of associates, which in turn depended majorly on front-line people managers.

- The essentially project-based nature of work meant conscious efforts would be required to ensure consistent people management practices across teams and leaders, important for junior-level associates to experience engagement across the organisation.

These priorities were ratified and refined by the annual 'Voice of Associates' survey and focus group discussions which featured over 250 associates, and finally gave rise to the launch of *'iZen—I Make Change Happen'*. The level of commitment displayed and communicated by the leadership ensured the entire organisation sensed the thrust being directed in this area; all stages of the initiative witnessed frequent reviews with the CEO—Dr Ganesh Natarajan, against clearly documented goals and action plans.

In order to make this initiative a more prominent and direct aspect of everyday work, the following organisational outcomes were identified as success factors for iZen:

- An increase in the engagement score, as determined by the annual 'Voice of Associates Survey'.

- Increase in employee retention rates.

- Far more engaged teams with project managers actively practicing consistent people management practices in the areas of building connected teams, development of team members and providing ongoing feedback.

- The onset of a parallel movement where individual Zensarians take responsibility of driving engagement initiatives that they are passionate about, thus providing freedom to employees while broadening the organisational scope of engagement initiatives for Zensar.

WORKING TO BE THE CHANGE THEY WANT TO SEE

The philosophy of iZen married the concepts of freedom and accountability as natural duals. The clarion call was 'I am Zensar', thus holding each associate accountable for the people, processes and systems at Zensar, whilst affording a sense of empowerment and freedom to make change happen. This phase (2011–12) witnessed the launch of the two key iZen prongs:

iZen Action Teams

These were formed within each Zensar Business Unit (BU)/ location (six in all), comprising associates from across levels in that BU. Each team included the BU and HR head and drove engagement initiatives for their BU. Outcomes of the focus group discussions held earlier in the year were shared with the iZen action teams who worked specifically on initiatives related to Fun at Work, Rewards & Recognition, Communication and Work Environment.

iZen Engagement Workshops

Were held for Zensar managers across levels—from Leadership levels to the Project Manager levels. As a result, all managers were driven to 'make change happen' within their teams by ensuring consistent people management practices. This was connected to the overall business goal of USD One Billion by 2016, keeping in mind the need to scale up the engagement agenda, drilling down to project manager level, in sync with the growth of the organisation and operations. These workshops focused on three key areas—building **connected** teams, providing ongoing **feedback** and creating clear **development** plans for team members.

Over twenty such workshops were held across Pune, Hyderabad, South Africa, UK and the US, covering over 400 people managers. The fact that these workshops were conducted by senior leadership, including the CEO, Business and HR Heads, lent great credence to the efforts and the key message being driven across was the need for managers to own and enhance the engagement and motivation of their teams.

The team took great efforts to drive the change forward, by clearly articulating action plans as outcomes of every workshop, focusing on the three pillars of connectedness, feedback and development. Additionally three structured follow-up sessions were conducted comprising knowledge and experience sharing through progress update discussions and presentations to the CEO.

This rigour and incisiveness of execution, together with the steadfast support of the CEO and leadership, all contributed greatly to the success of this multidimensional change effort.

MARKETING THE CHANGE FOR GREATER ADOPTION

Fully aware of the need to support such a change initiative with communication avenues to drive and reinforce desired behaviours, norms and leadership styles, the Marketing and HR teams collaborated to design and deploy an impactful communication campaign comprising teasers, posters, cascades, features in eZenscapes (the global newsletter across Zensar), focused contests and launch events at Pune and Hyderabad.

The rigorous follow-up sessions enabled the much needed feedback channel through the knowledge and experience sharing discussions. These interactions lent key insights on the efficacy of the workshop design, articulated action plans and communication channels, while also bringing forth practical challenges towards realising the desired change at ground level. The presence of the CEO in several of these discussions and presentations meant many problems met instant resolution, which could otherwise have delayed and impacted change adoption and internalization of key messages.

OVERCOMING OBSTACLES, ENHANCING EFFICACY

The active involvement of business leadership, including the CEO—Dr Ganesh Natarajan, at every stage of the change planning and execution meant that much of the generally expected resistance stood minimised. Additionally, the fact that business heads featured personally in the iZen action teams and engagement workshops made the core messages more relevant and digestible for the employee base.

The team went ahead and adopted an innovative step towards connecting with the leaders themselves. Aware of the common pitfall of taking leadership engagement and commitment for granted, an informal competition was organised for the best workshop facilitator based on participant feedback. Every workshop was followed by congratulatory mails to the leadership team reinforcing the importance of their sustained focus and energies for the change efforts to succeed.

The follow-up sessions described previously served to aid the change initiative on yet another front—identifying problem areas and change impediments proactively for immediate resolution. The presence of business heads and the CEO in these sessions greatly expedited efforts in this direction. These discussions and open interactions also helped build on early successes and positive energies, reinforcing the collective belief in the need for change embarked upon. The initial initiatives undertaken by the iZen action teams and early successes were publicised across Zensar, further adding to the momentum for change.

INJECTING THE CHANGE INTO THE ORGANISATIONAL DNA

Strengthening and sustaining the engagement had always been at the core of the change agenda. While the iZen initiative had taken the message right up to the level of front-line people managers, the progressive next step was to empower every individual Zensarian to 'be the change they want to see'. This was important to ensure real internalization and institutionalization

of the change, embedding it into the essential organisational fabric; and thus 'JUGNU' was launched.

JUGNU is a Hindi word for a Firefly and here the initiated 'JUGNU' referred to the 'inner glow' present in every individual. This initiative aimed at invoking the passion and joy associated with this glow translated in the organisational context and aimed at unleashing the passion for excellence in every Zensarian. Thus coined was the tagline—'Passion for Excellence—Ignited'.

Taking the idea of 'iZen—I Make Change Happen' forward, *JUGNU* urged all Zensarians to believe in and strive towards their dreams and bring their whole selves to work—passions and interests included. Work injected with such spirit was seen as driving actualization for the individual, while bringing in the excellence required for delivering on key organisational imperatives.

This focus on intrinsic passion and the pursuit of excellence was rooted in the fundamental belief that Breakthrough excellence cannot flourish consistently without engagement; nor can engagement deepen meaningfully without an individual pushing the boundaries of excellence.

With a focus to achieve the business goal of 1 Billion USD by 2016, this organisational frame of mind was essential for Zensar to function effectively as one large team, pulling together all employees to be bound by excellence and harmony. *JUGNU* also aimed at facilitating breakthrough, disruptive innovation, crucial for achieving results beyond the realms of steady, incremental growth.

In terms of branding, the name itself, *JUGNU*, was seen to be evocative and powerful in its connect with the inner glow and passion for excellence. The initiative was launched with the participation of hundreds of associates, at Pune first (November 2012) and then in Hyderabad (December 2012). Both launches were preceded by targeted teaser and communication campaigns. Additionally, the annual excellence awards event and the cultural extravaganza were both branded 'JUGNU—Passion for Excellence', thus reinforcing the call for all Zensarians to connect with their intrinsic passion and actualise at work.

Sustained Leadership involvement and endorsement

As in the case of iZen, there was full involvement of the Talent Management Committee (TMC), comprising business heads and HR heads. Once the concept was finalised, the first JUGNU workshops were held with the Strategy Management Council, followed by over sixty leaders from the top leadership group in both Pune and Hyderabad. This set the stage for the launch in November, post which, the TMC conducted regular progress reviews on next steps and overall efficacy.

Twelve 'hosts' were taken through a three-day Train-the-Trainer Program, equipping them to carry forward the JUGNU agenda within Zensar.

Execution: Leveraging Positivity and Generative Conversations

The ground-level execution of the JUGNU initiative was through excellence workshops, running in business units across the globe (at the time of printing). The excellence workshop was aimed at explaining the context of the movement and equipping associates to start working on their own ideas, thus benefitting both themselves and Zensar. The workshop design incorporated two powerful tools for driving and realising change:

Appreciative Inquiry (AI), encouraging participants to identify, connect with, and leverage their innate strengths to reach the desired state	Open Space Technology, providing a platform for people to gravitate towards ideas and initiatives of personal interest, and then work towards their implementation for desired outcomes

Through appreciative inquiry, each business unit went through the process of **Discovery**—the positives leading to excellence in themselves and Zensar, **Dream**—building a common vision for their business unit, **Design**— coming up with projects and action plans, and **Destiny**—implementing the action plans, post the workshops. The Design stage was conducted using open space technology, leveraging the power of a free platform to initiate discussions, ideas and subsequently projects which each person feels passionate about.

By using these tools of conversation and positivity in the workshop and outside, the *JUGNU* movement enabled Zensarians to joyfully contribute and grow.

These excellence workshops, co-facilitated by respective business heads are ongoing to cover all BUs and locations.

Each excellence workshop culminates in a clearly defined action plan, comprising organically designed and selected projects, based on personal interests and passions of participants. The timelines agreed upon and documented at this stage are tracked through active follow-up with excellence circles—platforms for sharing progress on the action plans. All participants are invited to the excellence circle and encouraged to share their journey so far and provided support required for the way forward. These sessions were hosted by the same business head who conducted the workshop, thus ensuring continuity, reinforcing leadership support and endorsement and maintaining urgency on the implementation of planned projects.

THE ENGAGEMENT IMPACT

While the iZen action teams designed and implemented several initiatives and ideas, the most notable among them was the re-ignition of 'ZenPoints', an idea that

> "Zensar has always been a 'connected' organization and the iZen initiative has enabled that culture to sustain and grow. The iZen workshops focus on connectedness, feedback and development, with sustained follow-up post the workshops as well. This enables better connect within teams and also between teams and customers. Another positive outcome has been that over ninety per cent of our project managers have clear development action plans with actionables related to both the individual's and Zensar's growth."
>
> **Dr. Ganesh Natarajan, VC & CEO, Zensar Technologies**

was initiated by a vision community years ago, but not taken forward at that time. This Rewards & Recognition scheme was eventually launched in April 2013.

2011–12 witnessed a seven per cent increase in employee retention over 2010–11, which has been sustained further, remaining well above the industry average, while employee engagement, tracked through the annual 'Voice of Associates' survey, rose by four per cent. By the end of FY 2012–13, over ninety-five per cent of Zensarians (from the CEO to the project manager level) had customised development action plans. Most importantly, business results exceeded targets on key parameters, holding Zensar in good stead for achieving the master goal of USD One Billion by 2016.

This chapter is based on the entry submitted by Ruchi Mathur (Head—OD and CSR, Zensar Technologies Ltd.), Janki Sampat (Manager—Industrial Relations and PR, Zensar Technologies Ltd.) at the Best Change Interventions of Asia Study 2012

What Zensar did differently to successfully manage and drive change

Zensar was successful in initiating and sustaining a movement that connected with employees across levels, invoking the innate drive for excellence and actualization. While this was a well thought out idea, its implementation would not have been successful without the following distinctive steps to enable the change effort:

• The active and unstinting involvement of the CEO through the entire process was undoubtedly instrumental in nipping many a derailer in the bud, and also key for reinforcing the value that the organisation saw in the programs.

• Another commendable aspect of the intervention was how it organically flowed from the success of the vision community initiative started in 2001, and is still thriving. That the desired change was 'evolution' rather than 'revolution', would have been evident from the way in which the essential life-giving forces of open, participative management and idea sharing remained constant throughout.

• Lastly, and perhaps most importantly, the manner in which Zensar managed to link business performance to the very core human attributes of passion, esteem and actualization, would be our one prime take-away from this fascinating story.

Lessons for Change Managers

The Zensar story presents the following key lessons for change managers conceptualising and driving interventions in organisations:

• In most cases, organisational and individual employee interests do not necessarily align by themselves. It is the test of a change manager's acumen, as to how (s)he identifies the real business ends desired (not symptoms/ paraphernalia), and connects them with what is genuinely valuable to the employee. Success at this core level ensures that the task of maintaining urgency and overcoming pockets of resistance is not limited to a select few members of the 'Change Management Team', but is instead a people-driven concern.

• Appreciative Inquiry can be useful in many cases where the change efforts could benefit from an initial boost of positive confidence in inherent organisational 'life-giving forces'. The approach of leveraging strengths to achieve the desired state can help minimise resistance while also enabling directed efforts at changing systems and structures as required.

- While the importance of leadership endorsement is a given for successful change, this story brings out how to go beyond paying lip-service on this front. Engaging with leaders without taking their involvement and support for granted, and leveraging their endorsement for maintaining both continuity and urgency, are key lessons one can take away from the Zensar story.

ABOUT THE BEST CHANGE INTERVENT-IONS OF ASIA STUDY

Launched in December 2012, the Best Change Interventions of Asia Study was the second independent study undertaken by the Learning & OD Roundtable, after the resounding success of the Best Learning Organisations of Asia Study, and Seminar event. The theme of change management was identified in keeping with the dynamic socio-economic and business environment that Asia finds itself in today. With the business challenges emanating from the global slowdown, unprecedented coupling among economies, and the subsequent dynamics relating to national and organisational cultures, the Asian socio-corporate milieu is rife with exemplary cases in the areas of change management, cross-cultural integration and organisational transformation. It is thus an opportune moment to document these experiences and learnings, in a manner that enables industry, academia, and society at large to evolve and prepare for the next level of business, social and economic challenges that await tomorrow. '*The Best Change Interventions of Asia Study 2012–13*' aimed to enable just that, by bringing out stories of successful and effective management and stewardship of change, in organisations across sizes, industry sectors and geographies.

The Study culminated in The Best Change Interventions of Asia Seminar and Awards event, which was held in July 2013 in Mumbai, where finalist organisations shared their unique change intervention stories with the jury and assembled delegates. The jury for the study comprised eminent experts from both industry and academia, including Dr T.V. Rao (Chairman—TV Rao Learning Systems and ex-Dean Indian Institute of Management, Ahmedabad), Anil Sachdev (Founder—School of Inspired Ledership), Mr P. Thiruvengadam (Senior Director, Human Capital Services, Deloitte), Prof. S. Ramnarayan (Clinical Professor of Organisational Behaviour, ISB) and Dr Kishore Dash (Associate Professor of Global Studies, Thunderbird School of Global Management).

Through the rigour of the detailed application and evaluation process, and the day-long seminar thereafter, the study succeeded in heightening the collective awareness of organisations on the key aspects of managing change successfully. For organisations that have been using variations/ partial aspects of the tenets of change management, the study enabled consolidation, benchmarking and refinement of the internal approach and practices, with sharper clarity on how to better align with and work through the following key steps in managing and leading change, along the lines of the seminal work of John Kotter on change management:

1. **Creating urgency around a vision for change**: Was there clarity on why the change was needed in the context of where the organisation was and where it needed to be? How was the vision for successful change created, and valorised among leaders and employees?

2. **Taking directed steps towards operationalising the change**: How was the backing of senior leaders and key influencers obtained? How were employees empowered to step up and participate in the change? How were diverse roles and responsibilities assigned and accounted for, for successful delivery on the change agenda?

3. **Designing a communication strategy and ensuring sound feedback mechanisms**: How were diverse employee segments oriented on the benefits from the change, to enhance buy-in? What feedback mechanisms were put in place to keep a pulse on the change initiative and its percolation across the organisation?

4. **Managing initial resistance and leveraging early wins to build momentum**: How was systemic resistance managed and overcome? How were early wins documented and leveraged in order to build momentum for the change agenda?

5. **Institutionalising the change to ensure it sticks**: What measures were taken to integrate the change into the systems and processes of the organisation? How was the change made sustainable and a part of the essential fabric of the organisation?

The above listed themes also formed the broad evaluation criteria for entries to the study. With a focus on specific change interventions, the study allowed organisations to apply with multiple entries (transformation stories) if they felt different interventions on their evolutionary journey merited documentation and discussion, and could add to the collective wisdom of the learning, OD, and larger corporate community as a whole.

The application format was as follows:

SECTION A—APPLICANT PARTICULARS

NAME	
JOB TITLE	
ORGANISATION	
TYPE OF INDUSTRY	
NUMBER OF EMPLOYEES	
ANNUAL REVENUES ($)	
ADDRESS	

CONTACT INFO	(O)	
		FAX:
	(HP)	

EMAIL	

SECTION B: ENTRY WRITE UP

Please provide specific examples with figures, charts, diagrams or any evidence to support your write up.

OBJECTIVE(S)
Please share a bit about your Organisation, such as: (**upto 200 words**) • Industry, products and services • Mission, vision, values and culture Please describe the external business environment and HR context leading to the germination of the change intervention, and the desired organisational outcomes/impact of the practice.

BRIEF DESCRIPTION OF MEASURES TAKEN TOWARDS
1. Creating urgency around a vision for change
....

BRIEF DESCRIPTION OF MEASURES TAKEN TOWARDS

2. Operationalising the change

....

BRIEF DESCRIPTION OF MEASURES TAKEN TOWARDS

3. Designing a communication strategy and ensuring sound feedback mechanisms

....

BRIEF DESCRIPTION OF MEASURES TAKEN TOWARDS

4. Managing initial resistance and leveraging early wins to build momentum

....

BRIEF DESCRIPTION OF MEASURES TAKEN TOWARDS

5. Institutionalising the change to ensure it sticks

....

IMPACT ON YOUR ORGANISATION

Please elaborate on the organisational impact of the above detailed change intervention, such as:

- Number of employees impacted
- Impact on employee, customer, organisational and financial measures
- Any endorsements from stakeholders (customers, suppliers, shareholders, unions, etc.)
- Strengthening of HR capabilities and processes
- Sustainable strategic benefits for the organisation in the long run

Please also outline factors which you feel contributed to the successful delivery of this impact.

ANY EXTERNAL ASSISTANCE

Please mention any external assistance received in any stage of the change intervention, such as the involvement of consultants, learning partners, etc. Describe the scope and depth of assistance provided.

Credit may be accorded for involving external experts in an innovative and thoughtful manner which complements the organisation's capabilities and strengthens overall results.

BEST CHANGE INTERVENT- IONS OF ASIA SEMINAR & AWARDS– PRESS RELEASE

Mahindra Rise declared winners at
Best Change Interventions of Asia
Seminar and Awards 2013
Awards showcasing business transformation across Asia

Mumbai, 4 July, 2013—The Learning & Organisation Development (L&OD) Roundtable, a knowledge-sharing and practice building forum for learning and HR practitioners, announced that Mahindra Rise was the winner for 'Best Change Interventions of Asia Seminar and Awards 2013', which was held recently in Mumbai. Capgemini won first runner up, whilst Wartsila, HPCL-Mittal Energy and Tata Motors were the second runner up at the event.

The results were the culmination of the Best Change Interventions of Asia study which focused on the theme of change management with the dynamic socio-economic and business environment prevalent in Asia.

Dr. Sujaya Banerjee, Founder, L&OD Roundtable said, "I would like to extend my congratulations to the winners of this year's awards. The objective of sharing these exemplary stories of change management and the learning insights that came forth, are to prepare the industry to manage the next level of business, social and economic challenges. The Best Change Interventions of Asia Study and Awards 2012–13 truly serve as a recognition platform for courage demonstrated through the twelve compelling stories of effective management and stewardship of change."

The keynote address was delivered by Dr Jayaprakash Narayan, MLA and Founder, Loksatta Party and Sudhir Vasudeva, CMD, ONGC, who spoke on 'Transforming India—How India can truly become a superpower'. Learning luminary awards were presented to Marshall Goldsmith, Founding Partner at Marshall Goldsmith Group, Ajit Rangnekar, Dean of Indian School of Business, Roy Pollock, CLO—6Ds Company, Sarah Cook, Managing Director of The Stairway Consultancy Ltd, Neharika Vohra, Faculty IIM Ahmedabad, Karie Willyerd, Vice President and Chief Learning Officer at SuccessFactors, Aroon Joshi, Founder and Professional Member of the Indian Society for Applied Behavioral Sciences and Arun Wakhlu, Executive Chairman, Pragati Leadership.

The seminar and awards was attended by over 250 HR professionals and CXOs across industries.

L&OD Roundtable, which is a non-profit society drives the cause of learning and organisational development across Asia and is committed to helping practitioners to build scalable and sustainable organisations.

VOICES @BCIAS

BEST CHANGE INTERVENTIONS OF ASIA STUDY

Some thoughts, views and opinions around the Best Change Interventions of Asia Study, Seminar and Awards event, as well as the stories of the participant organisations:

"It has been a great learning to go through various descriptions of change management initiatives of each organisation. I found a lot of genuineness in them. Small steps lead to big change."

—Dr TV Rao (Jury Member, and Chairman, TV Rao Learning Systems Ltd)

"You have set an excellent system for doing the evaluation work, and I really appreciate the seriousness and commitment with which you have gone about the entire process."

—S Ramnarayan (Jury Member, and Clinical Professor of OB, Indian School of Business)

"What made this process memorable is the ease with which one could navigate through the format. Very well designed, conceptualised and user friendly. Kudos to the L&OD Roundtable Team!"

—P Thiruvengadam (Jury Member, and Sr. Director—Deloitte)

"I am a great believer in the concept of knowledge sharing. I love what you are doing. I love the idea of professionals working together to help each other. I think we are all honoured to be in the Learning & OD Field.

—Marshall Goldsmith (Eminent Author and Thought Leader)

"I consider it a tremendous honour—I have watched with delight as the L&OD Roundtable has grown from a few dedicated learning professionals in Mumbai to a vibrant Pan Asian organisation with thousands of members dedicated to sharing best practices across India and the region."

—Roy Pollock (Chief Learning Officer—the 6D's Company, and Author of the Six Disciplines of Breakthrough Learning)

"I think what all of us need to do is to prepare for the next round of challenges and I am going to ask for your help to achieve this."

—Ajit Rangnekar (Dean—Indian School of Business)

"There's a saying in *Yoga* that the teacher in me honours the teacher in you and I hope you get the chance to learn from each other while you are there and I get a chance to learn from each of you."

—Dr Karie Willyerd (VP & Chief Learning Officer—Success Factors)

"This (Competency Based Interviewing) was a much needed and well thought out decision which immensely helped our recruiters to identify the right competency fit for a particular Sales role, especially in an environment where diverse geographic locations demand different flavours in competencies for successful sales performance."

—Vimal Vahi (Director & National Sales Manager— Dr Reddy's Laboratories)

"I honestly believe that the program has initiated the cultural change the organisation needed and with support and backing of our HR team, I am convinced that we will see better days ahead in career development at Capgemini. This journey has just begun and I am glad I am part of it."

—Ashutosh Misra (Head of Operations, Group Sales— Capgemini India Pvt Ltd)

"I have always believed that to be a successful leader, it is important to move out of the comfort zone. A leader needs to keep changing the environment around him. He should be open to ideas and should push himself into challenges and stretch to achieve them. The Transcend Program gave my team a push to break their silos."

—NS Bala (Sr. Vice President & Global Head, Manufacturing and Hi Tech SBU, Wipro)

"In any situation there are two important areas—the one which is in the circle of control and the other which falls beyond control. Understanding pretty well that there are many aspects where we have absolutely no control, team Wartsila chose to look at areas which can be impacted by them."

—Rakesh Sarin (Managing Director— Wartsila India Ltd.)

"Our teams have gone the extra mile to meet customer and architect community expectations and these success stories will inspire us to create new benchmarks. The RMX team through their efforts, discipline and team work have brought in better results with a strong focus on quality, production and service parameters."

—Frederic Guimbal (Managing Director—
Ready-Mix Concrete, Lafarge India)

"On the external side, the Mahindra brand now has a powerful differentiating idea—one that will help strengthen the brand in India and help establish it in global markets. It is through the idea of *Rise* that we hope to realise our aspiration of becoming a globally admired brand in the next decade."

—S.P Shukla (President—Group Strategy and
Chief Brand Officer, Mahindra & Mahindra Ltd.)

"The processes and systems along with the HMEL culture built during the program have enabled HMEL to ensure maximum utilisation of the assets."

—Harak Banthia (CFO—HPCL Mittal Energy Ltd.)

"Success is quite simple and the organisation which is successful, understands it quite well. The success story of PNBHFL is also quite simple. We did the right things in a simple way. The basics of implementation need to be correct instead of being complicated and this combination of being simply correct is what leads to success."

—Shaji Varghese (Business Head—PNB Housing Finance Ltd.)

"My sincere thanks and heartiest congratulations for organising the study and the awards. I can appreciate the long hours of work and thinking that it required and salute your team for their untiring efforts. Looking forward to greater accomplishments from the L&OD network."

—Sanjay Dhar (Sr. Faculty Member—
Management Training Institute, SAIL)

"The initiative (iZen) has been rolled out globally and contributes to building the next line of leadership, which is a critical requirement given Zensar's aggressive growth plans. We will continue to invest in iZen in the time to come."

—Ganesh Natarajan (VC & CEO—Zensar Technologies)

ABOUT THE LEARNING & OD ROUNDTABLE

The genesis of the Learning & OD Roundtable is a story I personally find quite fascinating, in retrospect and otherwise, and therefore see as worth sharing with the Learning and OD community. What is today the biggest professional forum in this niche, specialised area, started out as a motley group of 13 of us, Learning and HR professionals discussing and reflecting on the state of this field in the country, key challenges impeding its development and possible enablers. As one can imagine, a discussion among friends and colleagues on an area of passionate interest can last quite a while, and cover a rather esoteric mix of themes! From the many threads picked up in that extended dialogue, emerged a unanimously felt need for a platform enabling meaningful conversations, debates and discussions on the core challenges facing organisations, and the role Learning and OD professionals could play to address the same. While several HR forums existed and organised a plethora of events and seminars, a sense of 'community learning' was still missing wherein members could share insights from their experiences in driving change and OD agendas, focusing not just on what worked, but also on vital lessons to be learnt from failures. This need would form the core of our envisioned knowledge sharing forum, and remains a closely held value ever since.

The Learning & OD Roundtable was thus essentially conceived as a community of like-minded professionals in the areas of Learning, HR and Organisation Development, coming together to learn and grow as a whole. This spirit of 'everyone shares—everyone learns' lies at the heart of everything we do. The Roundtable serves as a knowledge-sharing and practice-building forum for Learning & OD and HR professionals, aimed at facilitating dialogue, building capability and sharing resources. In the last four years, the L&OD Roundtable has hosted various knowledge sharing forums, master class events, concept to practice sessions featuring renowned HR practitioners and subject matter experts, and two pioneering studies culminating in day-long seminars—the Best Learning Organisations of Asia Study and the Best Change Interventions of Asia Study. This will be an ongoing journey of excellence, which will recognise and celebrate best-in-class practices, for collectively raising the standard of L&OD practices in member organisations.

Currently serving over 5800+ members in India and abroad, this not-for-profit undertaking has chapters in Mumbai, Pune and Delhi, and has a

Governing Council comprising luminaries from industry and the academic world—Dr TV Rao (Chairman, TVRLS and ex-Dean Indian Institute of Management (IIM) Ahmedabad)), Mr Adil Malia (Group President HR—Essar Group), Mr Aquil Busrai (CEO—Aquil Busrai Consulting, Mr Shreesh Jamdar (Proprietor, Sambhav), Mr Prince Augustin (EVP Human Capital—Mahindra & Mahindra), Mr Rajeshwar Upadhyaya (Director, Par Excellence), and myself Dr Sujaya Banerjee (Chief Talent Officer & Sr. VP—Essar Group).

We have recently opened a chapter each in Pune (June 2013) and Delhi (August 2013) after much sustained demand. While members, colleagues and friends had been calling for this for over a year, we felt it best to let the forum stabilise and find its feet before expanding. Having done so, it is indeed very fulfilling to see the group grow, and more and more professionals joining in the spirit of collective learning and growth.

I would like to dedicate this book to all our members, who have trusted in us and come forward sharing fascinating stories and insights, and most importantly, joined us in our collective journey forward.

THE SWITCH CHANGE MAN- AGEMENT REPOSITORY

This section contains recommended resources that can be referred to by Strategic HR/ Learning & OD Practitioners to enable Change and Transformation Efforts within their organizations. While most of the mentioned resources are available in the public domain we recommend readers reach out to Individual Authors, Service Providers should they need additional details on the same:

BOOKS, ARTICLES, PUBLICATIONS

1. Kotter, J. P : Leading Change (Boston: Harvard Business School Press, 1996)

2. Brewster, Mike & Dalzell, Frederick : Driving Change (Hyperion, 2007)

3. Kotter, John & Cohen, Dan : The Heart of Change (Harvard Business School Press, 2002)

4. Conner, Daryl R : Leading at the Edge of Chaos (Wiley, 1998)

5. Cohan, Peter : You Can't Order Change (Penguin Group US, 2008)

6. Siegal, Wes and Stearn, Jonathan: Beat the Change Management Trap (Executive Forum, 2010)

7. Sugarman, Barry :A Learning Based Approach to Organizational Change : Some Results and Guidelines (Organizational Dynamics, Volume 30, No-1, 2001)

8. Prahalis, C.P : The Challenge of Change (Industrial Management, 1970)

9. Phillips, Julien : Enhancing the Effectiveness of Organizational Change Management (John Wiley & Sons, 1983)

10. Hannum, Mark : Ten Critical Factors for a Successful Change Initiative (Linkage, 2008)

11. Todnem, Rune : Organizational Change Management : A Critical Review (Journal of Change Management, Volume 5 No. 4, 2005)

12. Hartley, John, Benington John and Binns, Peter : Researching the Roles of Internal Change Agents in the Management of Organizational Change (British Journal of Management, Volume 8 , 1997)

13. Schaffer, Robert and Thomson, Harvey : Successful Change Programs Begin with Results (Harvard Business Review, 1992)

14. Cisco Systems : Change Management Best Practices (2008)

15. Queensland Government : Change Management Best Practices Guide

16. *Callicutt Chandra : Change Management Best Practices (TechExcel, Inc— www.techexcel.com)*

17. *Aiken, Carolyn and Keller Scott : The Inconvenient truth about change management : Why it isn't working and what to do about it," (McKinsey & Company, 2008)*

18. *Carter Eric : Successful Change Requires More Than Change Management (The Journey for Quality and Participation, 2008)*

19. *Denning Stephen : Using Stories to Spark Organizational Change (StoryTelling Foundation International)*

20. *Wursten, Huib : Culture and Change Management (Itim Intercultural Management)*

ExecBlueprints ™

*[Copyright: **Books24x7®**; The **ExecBlueprints** ™ are published as part of a subscription based service part of **Books24x7®** which provides concise, easy to absorb, practical information to help organizations address pressing strategic issues. For more information please visit www.execblueprints.com]*

1. *Ashford, Orlando , Cox, Dina and Campbell-: Change Management : Four Essential Steps to Provide for Smooth Transitions and Satisfied Employees*

2. *McHenry, Blake, Boyle, Judith A. and Donado, Yvette : Top Strategies for Individual, Team or Corporate Change Management*

3. *Cushing, Michael , Davis, Barry L , Kressel, Roberta , Dean, Virginia—The Only Constant : Mastering the Art of Change Management*

Guides, Checklists, Surveys and Toolkits

1. *SAP Organizational Change Management Toolkit (visit: http://scn.sap.com/docs/DOC-8040 for more)*

2. *Prosci's Change Management Planning Checklist (http://www.change-management.com/Prosci-CM-Planning-Checklist.pdf)*

3. *Spiro, Jodi : Leading Change Handbook—Concept and Tools (Wallace Foundation— Visit:http://www.wallacefoundation.org/knowledge-center/school-*

leadership/district-policy-and-practice/Documents/leading-change-handbook.pdf)

4. *Change Management Leadership Guide (Ryerson University, 2011)*
   Visit:http://www.ryerson.ca/content/dam/hr/management/change_mgmt/docs/ChangeManagementGuide_FINAL.pdf

5. *Siebel 4.0–2 Change Management Survey Questionnaire (http://www.questionpro.com/a/showSurveyLibrary.do?surveyID=352380)*

6. *Change Activation Toolkit (Better BusinessLearning) (http://betterbusinesslearning.com/change-management-methodology-compatibilities)*

VIDEOS/ TALKS

1. *Leading Change: Establish a Sense of Urgency (John Kotter—Kotter International)—*
   http://www.kotterinternational.com/books-and-resources/videos/view?ID=30523068

2. *Dealing with Resistance to Change (John Kotter—Kotter International)*
   http://www.kotterinternational.com/books-and-resources/videos/view?ID=30521646

3. *Six keys to leading positive change (TEDx Talk by Rosabeth Moss Kanter)—*
   http://www.youtube.com/watch?v=owU5aTNPJbs

4. *Change Anything—Use Skillpower over Willpower (TEDx Talk by Al Switzler, cofounder of VitalSmarts)*
   http://www.youtube.com/watch?v=3TX-Nu5wTS8

Note: *Learning Plus—L&OD Roundtable Advisory Services also offers (a) A two-days' program on Leading Change Efforts for HR Leaders (b) A two days' program called "Coming Unstuck—Overcoming the Challenge of Learning Transfer" for Learning/OD / Talent Mangers. For more details please write to INFO@ LNODROUNDTABLE.COM*

BIBLIO-GRAPHY

- *Kotter, J. P : Leading Change (Boston: Harvard Business School Press, 1996)*

- *Kamath, KV : India: A Story of Continuing Transformation (Vikalpa Volume 37 , No 2 , 2012)*

- *Conner, Daryl R : Leading at the Edge of Chaos—how to create the nimble organisation (John Wiley and Sons, 1998)*

- *Banerjee, Sujaya : No Pain No Glory—Leadership with Impact (Human Capital Magazine ,June 2012)*

- *Bhadoria, Vikas, Bhajanka, Ankur, Chakraborty, Kaustubh and Mitra, Palash (India Pharma 2020: Propelling access and acceptance, realising true potential, Mckinsey & Company, 2010)*

- *Schein, Edgar H (Organizational Culture and Leadership, 2nd ed. San Francisco, CA: Jossey Bass, 1992)*

GLOSSARY

A

AAI: Airports Authority of India *(From the GVK-MIAL Story)*

ACSP: Airports Company South Africa *(From the GVK-MIAL Story)*

Abhilasha 2015 (Abhilasha means Desire in Hindi): Change Intervention institutionalized at Lafarge with the objective of making Lafarge RMX the safest, most reliable and preferred business partner for the construction Industry in India *(from the Lafarge Story)*

B

BU: Business Unit

BDC: Bring Down Cost *(From the Wartsila story)*

BDC Times: Monthly newsletter published at Wartsila summarizing progress on each War Room Project. *(From the Wartsila story)*

Bubble Assignments: Action Learning Projects which helped participants of the Transcend program augment their understanding of the functioning of the business by working on real life business problems and generating solutions *(From the Wipro Manufacturing & Hi-Tech SBU story)*

C

Collaborative Business Experience ™ : Cloud-based, ERP independent, e-Procurement platform at Capgemini *(from the Capgemini Story)*

CBI: Competency Base Interviewing *(from the Dr Reddy's Story)*

CSIA : Chhatrapati Shivaji International Airport, Mumbai *(From the GVK-MIAL Story)*

Change Diamond—Conceptualized by IBM representing four key ingredients for driving change (includes Real Insights—Real Action, Solid Methods—Solid Benefits, Better Skills-Better Change and Right Investment—Right Impact) .This was leveraged by HMEL for driving change efforts around Project Prism *(from the HMEL Story)*

Cohort Based Normalization: With the object of avoiding the concentration of higher ratings at senior levels, Tata Motors leveraged PACT to ensure that the normalization process was conducted among peer-level employees only *(from the Tata Motors' Story)*

Coaching ImPact: Tata Motors launched 'Coaching ImPACT' in December 2012 to target People Managers across locations and units and help Managers have meaningful discussions with employees on their performance goals. *(from the Tata Motors' Story)*

COGS: Cost of Goods sold *(From the Wartsila story)*

CEA: Central Electrical Authority *(From the Wartsila story)*

D

Drishti-kon (in Hindi refers to perspective)—Employee Engagement Survey conducted for all GVK-MIAL employees as part of Change Management efforts *(From the GVK-MIAL Story)*

E

EXCELL: Executive Centre for Leadership Learning institutionalized by Capgemini India Pvt Ltd *(from the Capgemini Story)*

EXCELL+: Extended version of the EXCELL program for the Executive Leadership Team at Capgemini India Pvt Ltd *(from the Capgemini Story)*

EXCELL Lite: While the EXCELL program targeted the Vice President Population at Capgemini, up to one or two levels lower were covered under the EXCELL Lite Program *(from the Capgemini Story)*

Edgar Schein's model of organizational culture : Edgar Schein identified three distinct levels in organizational cultures (artifacts and behaviours, espoused values and assumptions). The three levels refer to the degree to which the different cultural phenomena are visible to the observer. *(from the Mahindra Rise Story)*

EBIT: Earnings before Interest and Tax

eZenscapes : Global Newsletter across Zensar

F

FY: Financial Year

G

Greenfield refinery: A refinery that has been built in an area where no previous facilities existed (from the HMEL Story)

GMCM: General Managers' Communication Meeting *(from the SAIL RSP Story)*

H

House of Mahindra : The core purpose of Mahindra Group was integrated with three Rise Pillars and Mahindra's core values to create the 'House of Mahindra'. Mahindra believes that the House of Mahindra inspires and motivates employees to achieve global excellence *(From the Mahindra Rise Story)*

HoD: Head of Department *(from the SAIl-RSP Story)*

HFO: Heavy Fuel Oil *(from the Wartsila story)*

I

IPP: Independent Power Plant *(from the GVK-MIAL Story)*

ISO : International Organization for Standardisation

INR: Indian Rupees

IDM : Integrated Document Management—the Internal Knowledge Management Portal at Wartsila *(from the Wartsila story)*

iZen: (I am Zensar) The iZen initiative was institutionalized for driving Freedom and Accountability and enlisting the participation and endorsement of all Zensar employees with the objective of enhancing engagement *(From the Zensar story)*

IDP: Individual Development Plan

J

JUGNU was conceptualized for Driving 'Passion for Excellence' as a lived value across the organization and bringing every Zensarian together in the shared quest for individual and organisational actualization *(from the Zensar story)*

K

Kotter's 8 Step Process for Leading Change : Harvard Business School Professor and world-renowned change expert, Kotter introduced his eight-step change process in his 1995 book, "Leading Change." The 8 Steps for Leading Change are as follows:—establishing a vision for change, creating the Guiding coalition, developing a change vision, communicating the vision for buy-in, empowering broad based action, generating short-term wins, never letting up and incorporating the changes into the culture of the organization.

KYB: Classroom module on 'Know Your Business' to drive on-boarding at Dr Reddy's. This was later documented by Dr Reddy's as a seven hour e-module, copied onto a CD and included in the Induction Kit for every lateral hire *(from the Dr Reddy's Story)*

KPI : Key Performance Indicator

Kshitij(which means Horizon) : Business Transformation Exercise institutionalized at PNB Housing Finance Ltd which incorporated best-in-class internal processes and policies to build capability and functional expertise among employees (from the PNB Housing Finance Ltd Story)

L

LEAD : (Learn, Enrich, Align and Deploy)—Structured Learning Sessions conducted for employees at GVK-MIAL on important behavioural and functional areas to build capability (From the GVK-MIAL Story)

LSIP: Large Scale Interactive Process used for Change Management and Execution efforts (used by Lafarge and HMEL)

LMS: Learning Management System

M

Multi Rater Perception Survey: One of the key components of the Diagnostic process of the EXCELL Program which was designed in view of the collaboration and team work necessary for success in a multi-geographic, multi-cultural environment like Capgemini *(from the Capgemini Story)*

MR: Medical Representative *(from the Dr Reddy's Story)*

MIAL: Mumbai International Airport Limited *(from the GVK-MIAL Story)*

MIALite : Recognition program to reinforce and role model desired behaviours and attitudes among employees at GVK-MIAL *(from the GVK-MIAL Story)*

miLEAP: Workshop conducted for GVK-MIAL by Mercer which culminated into the identification of relevant development areas for employees *(from the GVK-MIAL Story)*

Mahindra Rise: Rise is an external re-positioning of the Mahindra Brand and an internal cultural transformation to drive business out-performance at Mahindra Group. *(from the Mahindra Rise Story)*

MD's Post: Innovative e-mail based communication channel institutionalized by PNB Housing Finance Ltd to drive Change Efforts around Project Kshitij *(from the PNB Housing Finance Ltd Story)*

Maharatna: In 2009, the Government of India established the Maharatna status for seven PSU's and raised their investment ceiling from Rs. 1,000 crore (1.6 billion USD) to Rs. 5,000 crore (8 billion USD) *(from the SAIL RSP Story)*

MTPA: Million Tonnes per annum

ManCom : Management Committee *(from the Tata Motors' Story and the Wartsila Story)*

MW: Megawatt

War Room: Action Learning Projects institutionalized by Wartsila to bring down the Cost of Goods Sold. *(from the Wartsila story)*

N

Nine-box Performance—Potential grid : Grid used sto segment Talent Pools on Performance and Potential . This is actively used by a number of organisations during the Talent Review process

NPA: Non-Performing Asset

NPS: Net Perception Score *(from the Zensar story)*

New First Line Manager module : Deployed in February 2013 by Tata Motors to holistically develop first-time people managers on key capabilities crucial for fostering a healthy team ethic and high performance culture. *(from the Tata Motors Story)*

P

PSR: Professional Sales Representative *(from the Dr Reddy's Story)*

Parivartan (which means Change in Hindi):—Name of the mass contact program driven by GVK-MIAL as part of their Change Management efforts *(from the GVK-MIAL Story)*

Parivartan (which means Change in Hindi): An online listening post created for Tata Motors employees to share their comments, feedback, and suggestions on the existing PMS system as well as the new system which was to be conceptualised

Prism: Name of the umbrella program for implementation of business applications at HMEL *(from the HMEL Story)*

PE: Private Equity

PPP: Public, Private Partnership *(from the PNB Housing Finance Ltd Story)*

PMS : Performance Management System

PACT: Performance Assessment & Coaching Tool—The evolved Performing Management System with Coaching at its Centre *(from the Tata Motors Story)*

PAC: Performance Apex Committee to ensure greater transparency around normalization and calibration of ratings at Tata Motors *(from the Tata Motors' Story)*

PDCA (Plan-do-Check Action): This mechanism helped govern the implementation of PACT, reflecting a strong lessons-learnt orientation, drawing on 'Things gone right' and 'Things gone wrong' from the previous year's process implementation. *(from the Tata Motors Story)*

Q

Q1: Quarter One

R

Rightshore® : Capgemini's Global Delivery Model *(from the Capgemini Story)*

REACH : (Recognize, Empower, Align, Care, Honour)—Human Capital Strategy Model for GVK-MIAL *(From the GVK-MIAL Story)*

RSM: Regional Sales Manager *(from the Dr Reddy's Story)*

RSP: Rourkela Steel Plant *(from the SAIL story)*

S

SPARK: Employee Suggestion Scheme at GVK-MIAL *(From the GVK-MIAL Story)*

Star of the Month: Employee Recognition Program at HMEL *(from the HMEL Story)*

Samosa: Name of an Indian snack

SAP MES: SAP Manufacturing Execution Systems

SWOT: Strength, Weaknesses, Opportunity and Threat

Sutradhar: Common thread (in Hindi) *[from the Tata Motors Story]*

Sampark (Contact) : Innovative Communication Campaign institutionalized by PNB Housing Finance Ltd to drive Change Efforts around Project Kshitij *(from the PNB Housing Finance Ltd Story)*

Samskar (Cultural Heritage): As part of the Mass Contact Exercise at SAIL-RSP, regular meetings were organized between employees and the Top Management to encourage sharing of expectations, feedback, and concerns of employees. Each meeting would end with employees undertaking a pledge to build a sustainable work environment and commit to the success of the Rourkela Steel Pant. This pledge called *'Samskar"* later became the vision of the Rourkela Steel Plant. *(from the SAIL RSP Story)*

Samskriti (Culture): Refers to reinforcing a culture of safety, environment, quality and cost consciousness by converting awareness into action at SAIL RSP *(from the SAIL RSP Story)*

Samprasaran (Expansion): Refers to reaping the benefits of expansion by galvanising every mind at SAIL RSP *(from the SAIL RSP Story)*

Spandan (Vibrancy) : Refers to the objective of making every workplace at SAIL RSP a haven of vibrancy and fulfillment *(from the SAIL RSP Story)*

Samanway (Synergy): Achieving total synergy by creating a symbiotic relation with each valued partner at SAIL RSP *(from the SAIL RSP Story)*

Samvardhan (Sustainable Growth) : translates to cultivation, development, promotion, augmentation and enrichment of the SAIL RSP. It represents the aspirations of Rourkela Steel Plant *(from the SAIL RSP Story)*

Samriddhi: Prosperity (from the SAIL RSP Story)

Sankalp: Resolve (from the SAIL RSP Story)

SteCo: The Steering Committee for the War Room Projects who formulated the War Room Code *(from the Wartsila story)*

SBU: Strategic Business Unit

T

TTT : Train the Trainer

Transcend : Structured Leadership Development Intervention conceptualized and delivered to build a robust and agile Talent Pool of competent Senior Level Managers for Wipro's Manufacturing and Hi-Tech SBU*(from the Wipro story)*

TMC: Talent Management Committee to monitor progress of iZen and JUGNU initiatives *(from the Zensar Story)*

U

USD: US Dollars

V

VMV: Vision, Mission and Values *(from the GVK-MIAL Story)*

VALUE STAR: Employee Recognition Scheme at GVK-MIAL *(from the GVK-MIAL Story)*

VAP: Value Added Production

VC: The Vision Community initiative was launched in 2001 at Zensar. Through the initiative, Zensar offers all employees a medium to share their inputs, feedback on organizational strategy and key decisions *(from the Zensar story)*

Voice of Association—The Engagement Survey at Zensar *(from the Zensar story)*

W

Wheel of Change : The Wheel of Change was used to visually depict the roadmap for re-engineering HR Processes at Mahindra Group in line with the Rise philosophy *(From the Mahindra Rise Story)*

War Room Code: Guidelines for War Room Projects *(from the Wartsila Story)*

WIIFM: What's in it for me? *(from the Zensar story)*